WHO PUT THE KIDS IN CHARGE?

A FRESH APPROACH TO RAISING GREAT KIDS

SHARON CULLINGTON

Published by the Power Writers Publishing Group in 2021.

Sharon Cullington copyright 2021.

All Rights Reserved. No part of this book may be reproduced by any mechanical, photographic, or electronic processes, or in the form of a phonographic recording. Nor may be stored in a retrieval system, transmitted or otherwise be copied for public or private use other than for 'fair use' - as brief quotations embodied in articles and reviews, without prior written permission of the publisher.

 A catalogue record for this work is available from the National Library of Australia

ISBN: 978-0-6452108-0-4 (pbk)
ISBN:978-0-6452108-1-1 (ebk)

Cover and internal layout by
Publicious Book Publishing
www.publicious.com.au

Disclaimer

Any opinions expressed in this work are exclusively those of the author and are not necessarily the views held or endorsed by others quoted throughout. All of the information, exercises and concepts contained within the publication are intended for general information only. The author does not take any responsibility for any choices that any individual or organization may make with this information in the business. Personal, financial, familial or other areas of life based on the choice to use this information. If any individual or organization does wish to implement the ideas discussed herein, it is recommended that they obtain their own independent advice specific to their circumstances.

Contents

FOREWORD i
PREFACE vii
ACKNOWLEDGEMENTS xiii
INTRODUCTION xvii
HOW TO USE THIS BOOK xxix
MY STORY xxxv

PART 1 – Being a CALM parent
  CHAPTER 1: COMMUNICATION 1
    Noticing changes in your child's behaviour 3
    How to speak to children so they want to listen 8
    Stick to your word 10
    Make your requests a statement rather than
    a question 12
    Playing with words 13
    Use your imagination – or whatever it takes –
    to connect 15
    You can't raise kids without (sometimes) raising
    your voice 15
      Method 1 17
      Method 2 19
    How do you sound? 20

CHAPTER 2: ATTENTION 23
    It takes a village 23
    Make manners matter – notice what's going on 26
    What should families focus on? 28
    Be aware of being manipulated 29
    Sharing stories to encourage feelings 31

CHAPTER 3: LEADING 33
    What I learned at day care 33
    Everyone wants to be boss 36
    Beginning to eliminate what's not working 39
    How to restore and rebuild connections 40
    Respect 44
    Two things to focus on to get children to respect you 46

CHAPTER 4: MANAGING 51
    Managing feelings 52
    Managing changes 53
    Managing difficult conversations 56
    Managing your position as role model 57
    Managing discipline 58
    Managing self-control and consequences 61
    Managing the push back 65
    Managing aggressive behaviour 67
    Managing the love bug 68
    Managing the proceedings 72
        Scenario 1 72
        Scenario 2 72
    Managing readiness 75
    Managing decision-making 76
    Reward charts 78
    How and when to reward your children 79

Managing hovering and fixing 81
Managing instant gratification addiction 82
Managing manipulation 85
Manage your fear of being judged 88
Managing disrespect 90
Weekly family meetings 91
Managing sleep 95
Managing meal times 97
Managing tantrums 99
Managing hitting and biting 100
Managing teenagers and pre-teens 101
Managing moods and enabling respect 101

PART 2 – Seeing the family as a TEAM

CHAPTER 5: TRUST 109
Say what you mean and mean what you say 110
The importance of togetherness 111
Affection is what affection does 112
Working as a team 114
CHAPTER 6: ENJOYMENT 117
Enjoying looking after yourself 120
Have fun 122
It's okay to break the rules sometimes 122
Don't overcommit 124
Enjoy your children 125
Let your child know who they are 126
CHAPTER 7: APPRECIATION 128
CHAPTER 8: MINDFULNESS 135
Making the most of it 137
No need to be perfect 139

Keep it lighthearted if you can 141
Change your self-talk, change your life 142
Don't neglect self-care 142
Disrupting existing patterns of behaviour
within the family 143
Grab some 'me' time everyday 143
What if I don't feel like it? 147
Have a positive outlook 148

PART 3 – Getting your kids to play BALL
CHAPTER 9: BOUNDARIES 155
    Scenario 1 158
    Scenario 2 159
    Scenario 3 159
    Scenario 4 161
Keep things consistent 168
Keep a check on the messages you're sending 171
CHAPTER 10: AWARENESS 175
    Emotion regulation 181
    Kind and nice are great things to learn 186
    Change thinking 186
CHAPTER 11: LEARNING 191
    Tell stories 196
    Learning to do the things you don't really
    want to do 198
    Teaching our babies and children self-control 198
    Correcting bad behaviour nicely 205
    Teaching life skills 208
CHAPTER 12: LOVE 215
    Love is the most important thing 215
CONCLUSION 222

FOREWORD

I wish I had a book like this when my daughter was born. I was totally unprepared. Holding my beautiful baby in my arms for the first time was a massive wake-up call for me. The only problem was that I had no idea how to wake up.

I don't want to go into the myriad of lost opportunities in my own case, but I want to congratulate you for finding your way to this book. You're already on the front foot and you're going to be amazed at how simple it can be to set up a framework where everyone in your family can thrive. You'll notice I used the word *simple* and not *easy*. That's because not everyone who picks this book up is going to be the parent of a newborn and bad habits can be tricky to shift once kids get into the terrible twos and beyond.

But fear not. Sharon has been there and done that. She is sharing with you everything she learned as a mum and developed as a parenting coach over the last three decades.

Don't listen to me, though, listen to what Sharon's kids have to say about growing up with their wonderful mother by their side.

Jane Turner
Book Writing Coach

Vanessa, 38-year-old mother of a 4-year-old:
I remember when my son was about 8 months old and one of the other mums in our first-time mums' group was having trouble with her little girl throwing food on the floor. It seemed like a small thing, but she was earnestly asking for advice. It had gone beyond just messy weaning; it had become a game that only one of them was enjoying. When the other mums kind of shrugged and gave their best sympathetic smiles, all agreeing it was pretty normal, I was less convinced.

From day one, Mum explained to me that, as precious as this new baby was, I was at the beginning of a relationship that was going to be entirely different from anything I'd ever known. I was a teacher as well as a mum. It was a hard pill to swallow in those early months when all I wanted to do was show him how adored he was and treat him like a little prince. I couldn't wait to hear him say: I love you, Mummy.

But this wasn't about making a new best friend or being 'in love' again. This was a lifelong journey.

For River to be happy, I had to teach him how. And I did. The proof of my success as a parent would not be in how great he thought I was, but how well he settled into our family, and eventually the world. I soon realised I didn't need to accept anything as normal if it made my life unnecessarily harder. My husband and I had to decide what we would tolerate and what we wanted for our family. Not just now, but in the long term.

When our son started weaning at about 6 months, food throwing was off the menu. Not least because our dog is an incredibly efficient vacuum cleaner and a single grape could have killed her but because the idea of popping up and down from under the dining table didn't feel like fun. Being a parent is hard enough but being a source of entertainment at your own expense, or a punching bag, or a servant, or treated without respect and kindness – these things actually aren't in the job description.

Mum's parenting philosophy gave my husband and me the confidence to set our standards, to keep setting them and remind each other they're important because kids are so convincing. Four years in and we're both so grateful to Mum – not only because the tough days are rare, but I thank her for the good days when my clever, sweet boy holds my face in his hands, looks right into my eyes and says: I LOVE you, Mum.

34-year-old Oliver: I could happily write my own book about the unique and loving bond Mum and I have but for now, I just want to briefly explain how her strength in parenting helped me become the man I am today.

My childhood was a blissful experience. That probably had a lot to do with being raised by a lioness. Mum was confident, compassionate and always stood by her word. There was no question about who the boss was. As a young cub, I wanted to make her proud. Knowing there was mutual trust and respect in our pride meant the world to me.

I had freedom that most other kids didn't have. I knew Mum wanted the best for me. And more importantly, as a kid, I knew she wanted me to have fun. The respect we had for each other worked both ways. If Mum told me I wasn't allowed to do something, I knew she was saying it for a reason and I trusted it was for my own good. Mum used to say: No matter what you do, I will always love you, nothing will change that.

Knowing she was always on our side didn't mean she didn't hold us accountable when we did the wrong thing. Being able to do this, and never leave us in doubt about being totally loved, is a special skill that Mum had. I'd like to hope this is a common attitude parents have because it meant a lot to me as I was growing up, and it still does. I knew Mum was always there for me, no matter what. She always had my back, and I knew that, together, we would get through whatever mistake I made or whichever spanner life threw at me.

31-year-old Eloisa: Mum has given me the confidence to be myself ever since I can remember. I was encouraged to be playful, creative and entrepreneurial, and to always be kind to people (even the bullies at school). Mum's approach not only gave me the ability to understand why people behave the way they do, but it also enabled me to let go of negative feelings and move on as quickly as possible with a healthy perspective and sense of self-worth.

The way I see it, there are two types of attachment. There's the kind that breeds resentment, ego and loneliness, and the kind that is based on unconditional love, consciousness and truth. The latter is the kind of attachment that Mum and I share. She helped me to realise that life is full of fun as well as adversity and it's not the adversity that makes life painful – it's how we respond to it that counts. I'm grateful I was given the freedom to try things, to make mistakes and to come out the other end wiser for the experience.

It can be challenging to find the balance between independence and interdependence; however, Mum gave me all of the skills I needed to create autonomy and happiness. Mum and I share a unique relationship, at times our bond is so strong that I call her my best friend. Other times, her approach was so honest, raw and straightforward, that it bruised my ego. Once I had time to process and reflect on what had gone on, however, it was always clear to me that Mum was right.

Mum forgave us when we did the wrong thing, and we forgave her when she wasn't perfect because no-one ever is. There were never any grudges held. If we did something wrong there would be a consequence and a make-up cuddle, followed by laughter and more fun.

This has been a great way to learn about life.

PREFACE

This book is for anyone who is raising a child in all types of family structures. I will refer to you as 'parent' just to keep it simple but you could be a carer, friend or another relative.

Let's face it, when it comes to parenting, which we all know has been happening since the beginning of time, there's never been so much confusion and fear. This is due to a variety of factors – the most obvious of which is too much information. There's an abundance of conflicting online information out there. It's an easy trap to fall into. As the parent, you are the creator of your parenting style. It is the foundation on which your children will grow up. It determines the happiness of your family and who your children become as adults. Of course, you want to get it right.

I have written this book because raising great kids does not happen by accident – but it's not meant to be hard either. How you make your children feel as part of your family, and the kind of tone, energy and loving attention you give them, sets them up for life.

Today is the day we honour you because you care enough to keep searching and hoping to find out how to get the most important job of your life right. The great news is that it's never too late to be the best parent you could possibly be for your child. The important thing to remember, though, is you do not have to be the perfect person or the perfect parent. You just have to make sure you notice what's going on and do your best to fix things if they aren't working. Loving your children is the easy part.

The happiest, most well-functioning families I see are the ones where the relationships are respectful, and every member feels loved and understood. When you are consciously attentive to what is happening on a daily basis with your family and in your home, you can make changes when they are needed. That's when the members of your family feel happily belonging, without any need to provoke rudeness or disrespect at any age or developmental stage.

No child should have to slip through the cracks because nobody noticed what was going on for them when they were struggling. It would be crazy to leave something this important up to chance. These days, it's clear to most people that how we are raised determines how we feel about ourselves and affects many areas of our lives, including our mental health and self-worth.

There's a whole heap of parenting books, filled with research and statistics. This book is a bit different. I have written a parenting book as a parent who has almost 40 years of personal and professional experience, raising dozens of children one way or another.

Over that time, I've noticed there are some children who consistently improve their behaviour and are enjoying their lives. In the past, this was common. Today, it's not the norm. The fact is this – a well-behaved, happy child is the result of loving but firm parenting from people who aren't afraid to do whatever needs to be done to help their child achieve autonomy and reach their full potential.

Parents who consciously deal with their own 'stuff' first are better parents. Unfortunately, in our Western culture, there is an insidious and largely unrecognised habit of not learning how to deal with our emotions. We avoid them. We are encouraged to push them down and pretend everything is fine. As parents, sometimes we need to draw on our acting skills to get through some situations but we must also find the space and time to focus on freeing ourselves from auto pilot so we can really enjoy these precious moments. Otherwise, how on earth are we supposed to effectively teach our children to deal with their emotions?

The simple answer is – we don't. Instead, we give in to all the challenging behaviours and tantrums, trying to pander to their every need or complaint, just to avoid upsetting them.

I used to be that parent – the one who gave in; the one who ignored annoying behaviours. Now I see it happening a lot of the time in the families I work with. What we need to realise is the mental and physical wellbeing of parents and their children is never going to be healthy in this situation. We need to understand the importance of looking after ourselves first – because we matter. We must learn to parent without fear so we can stop giving in to our children.

How would it feel if you were a relaxed parent? What if raising your family were easier and your children were respectful and happier?

What I am sharing with you in this book is how I was able to finally see the truth, and what I did about it. I know firsthand what it's like to be fearful as a parent. Fear-based parenting, for me, was driven by a desire to be loved unconditionally by my first-born child. It was me who created a home environment that was unnecessarily exhausting; I didn't realise I was actually teaching my daughter to keep pushing me until I caved in. Not dealing with my own emotions first was essentially damaging my family dynamics – I know that now.

It was divorce and desperation that ultimately gave me the *wake-up call* I needed so I could see what was really going on. Only then did I realise I had to find some strategies to manage the difficult situation I had encouraged.

The greatest blessing in my life has definitely been my three beautiful children who taught me far more than I could have learned any other way. The grounding and guidance they (eventually) received from me shows up in myriad ways, not least in the bond they share and the loving support they give to me and each other through the fun times as well as the challenging ones.

I've written this book because I want you to utilise the benefits of parenting your children the way I have so you and your children can really enjoy this precious time in life. In this book, you can access everything I've learned and used in my parenting to help you with every stage of your parenting.

I believe having a structured and confident approach to parenting is the best way forward for all families. The stories, exercises and ideas I share in these pages will help you create a parenting style that suits you. The firm yet fun style I share in this book has helped many families, not only mine, to get out of chaos and under control so everyone feels loved, accepted and happy every day.

Living with children is not meant to be difficult. If you're anything like me, the idea behind having children was to experience more love, joy and connection in life. The great news is that it's never too late to create the conditions where this can actually happen. Opening yourself up to noticing things you couldn't see before is just the beginning of building a parenting style based on an authentic foundation where you'll start experiencing positive results almost instantly.

This book is designed for parents with busy lives. You can read it in just a few sittings, or perhaps in an afternoon, and you will soon discover every secret and strategy I used to get my own family running smoothly and happily. These are the same secrets I use when coaching parents who want to get off the dysfunctional family rollercoaster and on to solid foundations, helping children feel safe and parents to feel less anxious. I love it when the penny drops.

We can all be great parents. Everyone is able to create an environment where happiness and harmony is the *mode du jour* every day! It's never too late to be the parent your child wants AND needs.

ACKNOWLEDGEMENTS

Having enjoyed a life where I've been loved, adored, and appreciated by my children gave me the confidence to write this book. In fact, it was primarily written for my children, my grandchildren and their children. As an older woman, I feel like it's important for me to share what I know about raising children so my experience can be passed on and utilised. Writing a book is never easy and it's the support and love that gets you through it.

To my first child, Vanessa Violet, thank you. You have always been my test pilot. Being the first child has its own special challenges because parents have such high expectations of themselves and no road map to follow. You looked into my eyes, nodded your head and opened my heart the moment you were born, my beautiful Nessie. You taught me about unconditional love. You've achieved so much and we are all so proud of you, especially for choosing such a wonderful husband who we also adore. Thank you for the way you are raising my gorgeous grandson, River. He is a delight to have in the family and further proof children of all ages can be fun to live with. Thank you for your amazing input, wonderful ideas and your undying support in helping me edit, rewrite and curtail my ramblings as I brought this book to life, darling. You've been amazingly supportive and loving. You are always the one we go to when we can't work things out.

To my son, Oliver James, thank you. The cover for this book would still be a work in progress if not for you, Ollie. I asked you because you always know if something is right or wrong. And we managed to get everything done without too many words. Thank you for being the wonderful person that you are; always making us laugh and doing whatever it takes to keep the family happy and feeling supported. Thank you for setting me straight when I have the audacity to complain about life, especially all the whining about how hard it is to write a book. Your ability to make everyone feel heard and understood is just one of the precious gifts you give to the world and why you're often asked for advice. I don't know if you've noticed this, Ollie, but everyone you meet adores you and I know that will never change. The world needs more men like you.

To my youngest daughter, Eloisa Grace, our sweet angel, thank you. Your never-ending accomplishments continue to astound us. You never say never and you give everything a try. Talk about 'feel the fear and do it anyway' – you could write the book. Always without fanfare, you just keep moving forward. We are all so proud of you. I can't thank you enough for your undying support and belief that I could do this and for helping me to not feel lonely and isolated while I was writing. I will always be grateful for the way you shared your beautiful home with me, the massages and manicures you arrange for me, and for keeping me sane with amazing mini-breaks and never-ending cuddles from you and your puppy. All of this love and care kept me going, darling. When the going got tough, you got me through it. No wonder your clients adore you.

I also want to thank the people who, at different times over the years, inspired, helped, pushed and believed in me. Jane Turner, you got me over the line. You tirelessly and relentlessly filled in the gaps and pulled out the gems while encouraging me to do the same. You never entertained the idea of this book not happening. You told me you would be there every step of the way and you were, even minding the puppy when Ellie and I went away. Thank you, Jane, you really are outstanding and one of a kind. Moya De Luca Leonard, I am always in your debt for so much, not in the least your spirituality that inspires me to be better. Mary Szental, Oliver Sheade, Deb Hunt, Lance Miller, Maggie Hamilton, Karl Shaikh, Kelly Doust, Kellie Nissen – who all contributed whatever you could to help this book get to print.

ACKNOWLEDGEMENTS

I am grateful to all my friends and family members who encouraged me to keep writing because you believed this book would change lives. I especially want to thank my mother-in-law and friend, who will always be missed, Peggy Hurst, who showed me what a great mother looks like. To all the families I've had the pleasure of working with over the years – I want you to know you all made a difference but none more than all the darling children I've been blessed to have come into contact with and, more often than not, fallen in love with. I want to thank you all.

INTRODUCTION

As we begin this wonderful journey, allow me to be honest, right up front. I don't agree with passive parenting and giving in to kids. I've never seen any good come out of pussyfooting around children to stop them carrying on. What I know for sure, after working with children for so long, is they need to know who's in charge. Not only do children feel safe when they know who the leader is but they also know who to learn from and who turn to in order to understand life better. Children need to know there is someone they can trust; someone who knows what's going on and what's best for them. This allows them to relinquish the need to challenge you because they know everything is being taken care of.

Children feel a lot better when there are rules and boundaries in place. They also thrive on having clarity around what they need to do and how they should go about doing it. Relating to another person involves skills that can be learned and this book will show you how to speak to your children so they listen attentively. The beauty of this approach is that once certainty around trust and leadership is established, there is no longer any need for children to challenge the status quo all the time.

I believe it's important to constantly evaluate and re-evaluate how everything is going in all aspects of life – none more so than in the realm of parenting. I say this because being aware of what we are doing and the results we are getting enables us to jump in before things get out of control. For instance, nipping bad behaviour in the bud will stop behaviours turning into habits that we don't want to form.

My way of raising children creates more opportunities for fun to take place because you'll be less consumed with handling situations where the child wants to boss you around or ignore you. This is a more parent-empowered approach.

Parenting my children, and dozens of others, has been an ever-evolving experience of personal growth and love for me and all the children I've cared for. This book is for anyone who wants to really enjoy a lifelong experience of parenting with as many delightful moments as humanly possible – just as I have. Knowing you have a few useful skills and strategies up your sleeve makes that possible.

Let's face it, the world cannot promise happiness or stability. At any given time, you could lose your job, your friends, your spouse, your car, your cat, your house – you name it. So while you can't control everything, you can control a lot of what goes on in your home. By building a stable foundation and environment for your children to thrive in, you too will also love your family life. Parenting never ends, but I believe that when you raise your children with a good balance of firmness and playfulness, and invest bucketloads of love and attention, anyone can have a good chance at absolutely loving parenting.

Getting to that place is not about becoming the perfect parent. It's about being willing to be present, both physically and consciously. From day one, your child loves nothing more than having 100% of your attention and knowing they really matter to you. This is important because children are tuned-in to us. If we can't put the phone down to 'be' with them when we're spending time together, then they are likely to react adversely in a variety of ways. Imagine how you would feel if you had to constantly compete with a device when you were with someone you love. You would probably want to yell at them.

I cringe when I see parents allowing devices to come between them and the people they love. Screen addiction has the power to destroy precious relationships as well as giving our kids a warped sense of reality. I truly believe this is what's at stake here.

If you feel like you might have fallen into the trap of screen addiction, or worse still, if your children have, I want you to know you can begin to only use your phone when you need to, rather than most of the time. I'd really encourage you to do that, and to get help if you need it, because any addiction weakens our inner strength, decision-making and willpower.

This is an important point because your children watch everything you do. Whether you know it or not, you are teaching them to be just like you. I know change can be a scary thought for us to get our head around but let me assure you, it can be done. Helping children and adults change their problematic habits and behaviours is what gets me out of bed in the morning.

Being nervous about change is completely normal, especially if we feel as though we are stepping out of our comfort zone. It's easier if your comfort zone, which is really just an established way of thinking, gets used to being stretched. Just like any muscle, stretching might hurt a bit at first but then it starts feeling good.

I care about you as the parent but I care even more about your beautiful children. Raising children is a constant balancing act and often requires us, as parents, to modify what we're doing. It really bothers me when I hear people say that children today are disrespectful and rude – poor kids, it's not their fault. It's much more empowering, for everyone, to look at the current parenting issues, including too much conflicting information, and see this so-called rudeness is actually a result of children not knowing how to behave.

Let's face it – things in your family can only change when you do. Until you do change, they will more than likely get worse with time. In fact, I'm pretty sure this is something you would have already witnessed.

All teams need leadership but I'm not suggesting you adopt an authoritarian style of leadership. I teach parents how to have fun, yet also be strong when challenged. It's more about helping children with CALM authority and awareness. If you don't think leadership is important, ask any teacher how they feel about parents and discipline these days.

I've noticed news articles increasingly reporting the statistics around parents defending bad behaviour at school and making excuses for their children, rendering them unaccountable. Any store or café owner will eagerly tell you about children being allowed to run around out of control, touching everything and annoying other patrons while their parents seem oblivious and then become defensive should anyone say anything. This lack of boundaries bleeds into the home and all other areas of children's lives.

We all want happy children who are learning and growing into happy adults but one does not automatically result in the other. If we assess the situation without our rose-coloured glasses on, we will notice that being out of control is not helping our children be happy. Many kids today, whether small or big, are moody and bossy. It's clear that children in general are being hindered by the lack of respect for their parents, objects and other people.

Qualities such as resilience, courage, self-control and patience are easier to learn when we are made accountable for outcomes. And they are easier to teach when there is consistency and a clear set of standards to live by that are communicated and understood.

Let's also be clear that when you start consciously observing what's really going on in your home and realise what the long-term effects of not changing are likely to be on your children, you may get a real wake-up call that may make you a bit uncomfortable. However, I'm hoping to stimulate your curiosity so you will feel open to new habits, bringing a greater level of harmony and peace to your family life. Please don't lose heart. Instead, congratulate yourself for crossing the threshold to becoming the parent you feel proud of being.

The way forward is all about switching off autopilot. Your resistance to change will tell you how deep into the groove you are. Sometimes ignoring things is easier but wouldn't it be better to open your mind to a new range of possibilities by having fun with your children and being respected by them? Life is a game, as some say. Wouldn't you agree that being aware and prepared to change whatever isn't working is how you can position yourself and your family to be winners in the game of life?

Imagine how you will feel when your children have the confidence and the presence to look people in the eye whenever they are being spoken to, patiently excuse themselves when they need to interrupt someone and always say please and thank you when appropriate. How will you feel when your children stop thinking the only way to get your attention is to push back and trample over you and the boundaries?

It's a wonderful thing to see your children transform in front of you, watching as they become more confident about *positively* contributing to family life from a place of worthiness and gratitude.

I have seen miracles happen when parents become CALM leaders.

Being a CALM leader begins with gaining composure when your children push your buttons, or when you are feeling overwhelmed or tired. What you'll learn here is to have confidence in your ability to gain your children's respect so they will stop challenging you and begin trusting that you have their interests at heart, as well as your own.

Once you begin communicating in ways that open your children's hearts and minds to learning from you, rather than the false sense of power they get when they ignore or challenge you, life for everyone in your family will become a whole lot easier and more enjoyable. Imagine how life will feel when everyone in your household is coming from a place of solid connection – where everyone feels loved, respected and capable. That's when you can say goodbye to conflict and pushback and hello to genuine connection and cooperation. Believe it or not, I can guarantee your children will love you even more because of it.

Over the decades I've spent working with families, I have developed and refined a simple '7 Days to Well-Behaved' program, which shows parents the steps needed to achieve mutual respect and eliminate challenging behaviours. It all leads to a healthy and happy living environment for all family members. I am sharing all of this information with you to explore with your family.

Once you get the hang of the process, you won't have to pour huge amounts of energy into wondering what to do and how to implement change. In fact, being an empowered parent will actually result in a lot less work for you once your child understands what the expectations are and how to meet them. What's more, there will be less arguing, less exhaustion and less resentment when everyone begins contributing to the family and to running the home.

I want you to just pause for a moment and think about how it would feel if pleasant conversation was to replace the yelling, moaning and complaining from members of the family. If you find that hard to imagine, I'd like you to picture this scenario:

You're having dinner in a local restaurant and can't help but notice there are children almost the same age as yours at another table. These children are well-mannered. They sit nicely. They eat their food with cutlery. Nothing is landing on the floor. Nobody is complaining. Everyone is engaged and enjoying their meal together. They are talking and laughing, with not a device in sight.

This can be your family!

Perhaps it seems a little fanciful, especially if that scenario doesn't remotely resemble what's going on during a night out with your family at the moment. If so, try casting your mind back to what it was like when you were a child growing up. You may recall most families spending time together without arguments or devices. In the past, most families sat down to eat dinner at the table and enjoyed connecting and communicating.

Nowadays, many children show little or no respect for their mum and dad. I've seen children, from tiny toddlers through to teenagers and beyond, being verbally, and even physically abusive, towards their parents. This is more common than many of us would like to admit but let me assure you, as common as it is, it's not normal.

The real problem is that parents are busy and tired, plus they're confused by all the conflicting information available. It's little wonder we often lack the confidence or the energy to attend to bad behaviour when we are not sure what we should be doing.

It is, however, important to realise that children who are often out of control, or who don't listen and respond when spoken to, are not 'bad' kids. Rather, they are desperate to be seen and heard and have simply not been taught how to behave in a way that they 'get'. No-one wants to be in trouble all the time – least of all our kids.

Please don't go into overwhelm if what you've just read feels like I've just described what's happening in your home right now. I know what I know because, for decades, I've worked with countless families who are experiencing these same difficulties. I also know, without a doubt, family life doesn't have to be that way.

It's time for change!

My mission is to put an end to this kind of needless suffering for as many families I can.

The information I share with you will show you that *you* have all the resources you need to do something about the situation you are in. It's important you take this on board because things will only get worse if you don't do anything different.

What you can do from today is *take charge* and gain the respect you deserve. Open up to all the choices you have and the new decisions you can make today. Don't make the mistake of thinking parenting is about what the children want. It is not 'them versus us'. It's far more than that. Parenting is about establishing a mutual understanding of where everyone sits in the family, being a CALM leader and ensuring that no-one is overlooked. This family needs to work for every member, including yourself and your partner. You're the ones who can make that happen and its important, whether one parent or two, that you commit to being consistent.

What I know for sure is families don't need more technology, more philosophy or more theories. What families do need is more *connection* with the people who really matter to them. They need to rise above and see the blind spots. They need to stop making excuses and wasting time on things that don't matter so they can invest their time on things that do.

Here is it again:

- *Wake up* to see the blind spots.
- *Slow down* because your family needs you to be present.
- *Take charge* because every great team has a great leader.

Wake up – slow down – take charge.

That's it in a nutshell.

HOW TO USE THIS BOOK

This book is about family relationships in general, how you can help your children to be the best version of themselves and how you can enjoy every stage of parenting. Right up front, I want you to remember, this is not just about your children, it's about you too. To get the most out of this book, it is best if you can be open to the possibility of change and know you may have to get a little vulnerable.

Brené Brown, a masterful studier of 'authenticity' among other things, always reminds us of the importance of being vulnerable if we are to be truly happy and have authentic relationships. I'm reminding you as well. Vulnerability means being real so you can engage with yourself and the people around you on a deep and meaningful level.

We all build protective walls around us that others cannot penetrate. Strangely enough, we are often not consciously aware of them. When we are 'reminded' by those closest to us, we think or say something like: This is just me. Is it really? In my personal experience, having a family has been so life-changing that I wouldn't know where to begin describing it. Personal growth has been happening to me on a daily basis since becoming a mum.

This book, which has pushed me way out of my comfort zone, is for my children and their children more than for me. They have all contributed to its development in many ways. Luckily for me, they had a mum who showed them how to happily, and graciously, do the things they didn't really want to make time for. Attitude is everything.

Your kids, too, will help you to continue growing and will not allow you to get away with not connecting deeply with them. At the very least, they will do their darnedest to bring out the best in you – as well as the worst.

I'm telling you this because anything meaningful, like becoming a better person, is real change that doesn't just happen on a surface level. It happens deep down in your heart and soul. There's a good chance you haven't been to those deeper places for a while, and maybe you don't even want to go there now. That's okay for now. There are plenty of strategies and reminders in this book to help you to understand. You can't just read a book if you want to make a big difference to the way everyone in your family feels about being a part of your family. It's best to take your time so you can stop, ponder, recognise and see what is missing in your parenting and what you can do about it.

If you try my strategies to regain the leadership role in your family and you teach your children how to respect you and themselves but it's still not happening the way you want, try ramping it up by adding more undeniable, unequivocal, bountiful and loving moments of just 'being' together.

I encourage you to use this book in a way you feel comfortable. Begin the journey and start making a big difference to the way it feels to be you in your family. Remember that at the base of every strategy is more love. Apart from creating a deeper loving bond, please feel free to accept or reject anything I recommend. No two families are exactly the same and this is about you really getting to know the members of your family more deeply than anyone else.

That said, there are more similarities than differences when it comes to families who are finding it hard to connect and get kids to listen. I'm guessing you bought this book because you want to find a way to stop struggling with your children's behaviour and so you can enjoy more harmony and joy in your home. With your purpose in mind, don't get stuck on anything that doesn't resonate with you in the pages that follow but when you read something you think could possibly help, commit to giving it a go.

If you only get one tip out of this book and find that helpful – wonderful. However, there is also a lot to think about here. Inside each chapter you will find no-nonsense, fun and playful approaches to improving how it feels to be part of your family. My way of raising kids is based on the belief that every child wants to be good and deserves to know how.

You may be wondering whether getting things right means there is only one right way to be a great parent. Or you might worry about whether you've got what it takes. Don't worry, everyone can do all, or some, of what's suggested here. What I want is for you to relax and be prepared to get a little bit uncomfortable. I promise it will be worth it because once you come out the other side, you'll have a new perspective and a toolbox full of new strategies. You are going to feel a lot better about your life and your role as a parent.

This easy-to-follow parenting style is based on three simple acronyms to make the foundational points easy to remember and use.

- **CALM** parent who leads
- Family **TEAM** who work together
- Children who love playing **BALL**

This book follows the acronyms CALM, TEAM, and BALL to make everything easier to remember.

CALM

- **C**ommunication (Chapter 1)
- **A**ttention (Chapter 2)
- **L**eadership (Chapter 3)
- **M**anagement (Chapter 4)

TEAM

- **T**rust (Chapter 5)
- **E**njoyment (Chapter 6)
- **A**ppreciation (Chapter 7)
- **M**indfulness (Chapter 8)

BALL

- **B**oundaries (Chapter 9)
- **A**wareness (Chapter 10)
- **L**earning (Chapter 11)
- **L**ove (Chapter 12)

Throughout the book, you will find questions to help you apply what you've read to your family situation. This is a perfect opportunity to start to feel more empowered and experience more enjoyment in your role as a leader and parent. Take the time to answer these questions. Please don't miss out on this opportunity to reflect.

You will notice lots of repetition throughout the book which I have done on purpose. It is for the purpose of helping you to realise the importance of those messages, ensuring they are not overlooked or thought of as insignificant.

Be kind to yourself as you work through this material and reach out for help if you need it. I am only ever an email away.

MY STORY

Many years ago, before the divorce that changed everything left me as a suddenly single, working mother of three, my life was becoming increasingly unmanageable. My first child, Vanessa, believed she was the king and the queen of the castle, and acted accordingly. I defended her bossy behaviour passionately and put it down to her superior intelligence. Two more children and many years later, I realised that rather than the behaviour I was always defending being her fault, it was entirely mine.

That was a huge *wake-up* call for me.

In those days, the limited amount of time and energy I had left after work meant I was not prepared to say 'no' to Vanessa in case she got upset. I was not being conscious or noticing what was really going on and I didn't have enough experience to understand I was encouraging my perfect baby to develop bad habits.

My husband and I had grown apart beyond repair and the business we owned together was going downhill fast. I was running on adrenaline and living in survival mode. On top of this, being a mother of three children meant I simply didn't have the time or brain space to think about the long-term consequences of anything. What I know now, after nearly four decades of practical experience with my own family and others, is many parents are also operating in survival mode.

I had a moment of truth one day when a mum from Vanessa's school stopped me to say: You should take the time to smell the roses, you know, ponder. At the time, I was running up the driveway carrying my new baby, Oliver, while he was screaming for a feed. The first thought that popped into my mind was: Are you mental? Her timing was off, but her words stuck with me.

I was exhausted – mentally and physically drained. I was struggling to get through each day, running a business I was trying to keep afloat, with no support from my husband. In that state, it didn't even occur to me that that this mother was actually trying to help me to *slow down*. Through my haze of exhaustion, I thought she was just criticising me. So, I decided to hate her and keep running. However, I did think about what she was trying to say later that night as I was nodding off to sleep.

She had planted a seed and it was the nudge I needed to realise what was going on. Other people were noticing but I was too exhausted and focused on survival to *wake up* and actually, see what wasn't working. That moment of reflection resulted in two important things happening:

1. Goodbye, bad husband.
2. Hello, good kids.

This actually happened but it wasn't as quick or easy as it may seem when you read those words on the page.

I began observing myself to see what my children saw. I noticed things that I was excusing about myself, not in the least my automatic habits that were not helping us. I became aware of how I was thinking and acting around the children, which helped me to realise that I could be a better parent in a lot of areas.

That way of being for me was how I was able to pick up on everything that was going on for us as a family. For example, if any of the children talked over me or didn't look at me or respond if I spoke to them, I knew something needed addressing. In the early days, I would have ignored it or if I were stressed, I would have said things like 'Haven't I told you before?' 'Why aren't you listening to me when I speak to you?' And it would usually be accompanied with a head shake, eye roll or a following statement such as 'Why don't you listen?'

Observing myself, knowing I could do better, I decided to change from unconscious to conscious by being in the moment. I started to see how the things I was doing and saying to the children was not helping them to be the best version of themselves either. Like any habit or addiction, at first it's really hard, you'll get withdrawal symptoms and you'll want to give up. Still, like anything worthwhile, concentration, commitment and repetition is how you get over the barrier. Then it's easy as you've managed to form new habits.

We get so attached to being ourselves, forgetting that nothing is set in stone, and everything is just energy that can be transformed, and this includes, how we think and act.

As parents, we are on this growth path as much as our children are. Teaching our children, rather than doing things for them, is difficult. In my case, I was also in my head, ruminating and worrying, and I wasn't paying attention when my children were interacting with me. It took some concentration at first, but soon, being a hundred per cent with my children became my new habit.

A habit is just part of a set of behaviours. It often comes about unconsciously and is mostly developed by watching our parents. For instance, when parents bite their nails so do the children more often than not. However, as adults we are all able to take responsibility, notice what's going on and with a bit of effort, change whatever we need to, to get the results we want.

As a busy retailer, all day I was interacting with customers, haggling with manufacturers and managing staff. The last thing I wanted when I came home, exhausted, from work was more chitter-chatter from eager kids. However, I realised that if I wanted my children to learn how to enjoy doing the things they really didn't want to do, I had to model that behaviour for them. I learned how to flick a switch and go from retailer to mum.

Arriving home each night, I would ask the children about their day, and I made sure I listened attentively and playfully. I made their stories sound adventurous and sometimes suggested ways they could look at doing or saying something that may have made their day more enjoyable. I would actively engage with them. I showed them I loved being with them and found them fun and entertaining. This might sound like a little thing, but it really started to shift the dynamics in our home.

Establishing that kind of consistent and timely connection just before bedtime and really 'being' with the children was the beginning of a change in them. Suddenly, I had children who were looking at me and listening when I spoke without answering back or ignoring me. Soon, whenever I asked them to do something, they happily complied.

However, I had to learn to be strict with myself. I was so busy being busy and just doing things for them, usually because it was quicker. Finding the patience to explain what needed to happen was something I had to learn, and I admitted to the children that this was hard for me. We also spoke a lot about how things needed to change. I encouraged everyone to make suggestions and share collaboratively whenever possible but knew and reinforced that I had the final word.

Not only did I make sure there were well-understood consequences, but I also applied them with consistency when the children veered off track. As a family, we referred to these consequences as learning opportunities. Consistency was key. Essentially, I was retraining the children – out of their bad habits and into good ones. Your child's personality will help you decide what type of consequences will help to motivate them.

I needed children who were respectful and happy to contribute. I also needed them to be aware of how their behaviours affected those around them. Sibling rivalry was almost entirely eliminated, and we worked together as a TEAM. It was win–win.

Believe me, I made my fair share of mistakes, but I came to absolutely love parenting as a single mum. So much so that I eventually studied Early Childhood Development and became a professional Nanny before moving on to working as a Parenting and Family Coach.

That was almost 20 years ago, though it seems like only yesterday. Why? I found the magic formula and now I want to share it because I honestly believe helping parents raise conscious children and helping children to appreciate their parents is what I was born to do. Sometimes, I really need to shake things up, disrupt patterns of behaviour and do whatever it takes to help as many mums and dads as possible to find the skills that give them a great experience when raising their children.

One thing I know is that change is not easy for most people and doing things that may not come naturally can feel pretty uncomfortable – at first. But I want you to know that being prepared to push through any feeling of discomfort is going to be the key to fixing anything that is not working in your family as is realising that the discomfort is temporary but the positive results are for life.

I believe we need to *wake up* as a society and acknowledge that way too many families are stressed and struggling. We need to tell the truth and be real with each other. We need to get out of our heads and off our phones so we can start to really enjoy our families. We all want to enjoy parenting. Every effort you make now to get everyone on track is an investment in you. Quite frankly, the alternative is too stressful and unnecessary, as I'd discovered.

I love that moment when parents realise they are actually not that far from the place where balance can be regained. This place is where everyone happily enjoys their role, feels supported and loved and really loves family life.

There is essentially no difference between the kids who behave well and those who don't. Sure, some children are predisposed to being a little more boisterous or independent of mind than others but all children are fundamentally decent, loving beings who are programmed to push boundaries as part of their development. What's more, it is our job as parents to establish and maintain healthy boundaries our kids feel safe within, while still allowing them to grow and develop at an appropriate rate, regardless of the child's opinion of when that is. Remember, you know better – you're the adult.

I have never seen children hindered by loving and firm leadership. Nor have I seen a child hindered by pushing themselves to do the things that may not come naturally to them. However, children are disadvantaged by missing out on learning opportunities that teach them things like self-control, appreciation and the value of being respectful.

The time to take action is now.

And why wouldn't you? You love your kids.

PART 1

Being a CALM parent

CHAPTER 1: COMMUNICATION

*Only through communication can
human life hold meaning.*
— Paulo Freire

Good parenting starts with simple, loving communication. Get this right and you will find your children don't only want to hear what you have to say, they will also be confident in their ability to communicate how they are feeling, without acting out or disconnecting.

It is never too early to learn how to express ourselves so people want to listen.

One family I worked with had a very cute 3-year-old boy who walked around saying the same thing over and over. I noticed he was actually trying to communicate to his parents but no-one was listening. You see, he didn't know how to get the attention he needed to begin so he just began. This became a habit which caused his parents to think he just liked talking to himself. It took a few days but I showed Jimmy how to:

- say the name of the person he wanted to speak to
- look at their eyes
- speak in a 'big boy' voice so people could hear.

Once he learned these three skills, he soon stopped wandering around the room talking to himself and feeling unheard. His parents also realised they had to look into his eyes and wait to hear what he had to say.

The ability to communicate is so important for children because it stops a lot of their frustrations. For instance, a small child who has been hurt by someone's actions or words can carry that feeling in their little bodies for a very long time. Eventually, it makes them ill. They may respond by becoming naughty at home or at school or by doing things that hurt themselves or another child. If they knew how to tell you how they felt, then these things could be avoided.

It's important to keep lines of communication with our children open. Needless to say, this includes listening as well as speaking. As adults, we need to ask children questions and encourage them to speak. This may not be as easy as we would like. If we are stressed or busy, it could even be difficult. If that's the case in your home, trying a little harder to just get a response of any kind, such as a nod or eye contact, is enough to begin opening your children up to the process.

Our job as parents is to create opportunities for kids to feel they can open up to us. This won't happen unless you create an environment where they feel safe, free of judgement and supported. Active listening by reading body language and tone of voice will help you to know what's really going on for your child. Accepting 'I don't know' as an answer will only encourage your child to be silent, when they obviously need to learn how to communicate, so keep pushing until they make an effort.

You may like to share something about your day first and then ask about their day. Who knows what's likely to come up? For example, your 10-year-old may have been bullied by someone she likes at school and feel at a loss when it comes to knowing how to handle the situation. She may feel embarrassed, weak or some other version of what happens when we feel disempowered. Only you can help her with this so don't let her down. Let her know that whatever she is feeling, you can help her do something about it.

Noticing changes in your child's behaviour

This brings me to the importance of managing our mood so we are open enough to notice what's going on with the ones we love. It comes down to knowing your child well, tapping into your intuition and being aware and observant. This is impossible if stress and bad moods get in the way.

CHAPTER 1: COMMUNICATION

When kids are acting out, it's usually because something has happened to upset them. Rather than getting triggered and reacting, it's worth communicating to your child that they are safe, but that you've noticed they might not be feeling safe. Depending on how they react, you might go on to remind them they are never alone because you are there to help them whenever they need it.

Everything you say – good and bad – can become your child's inner voice. Being aware of your responses and trying not to blame or criticise is very important to how your children feel about themselves. What your children need to know is they will always be fully understood and fully supported.

Support is the best gift you can give your children. Undivided attention and care works wonders because it's only then your children are likely to start opening up to you. Don't worry if you haven't yet managed to set up an environment where this kind of loving and non-judgemental communication can take place. It's never too late to start.

Don't assume children know how to share their feelings with you or know how to describe exactly what is going on for them. They learn these skills by watching and listening to you and by having you encourage them to feel their feelings and express them if needed.

They might hate this process at first but they'll thank you for it in the long run. Always push through their unwillingness to talk to you by insisting they try.

If this doesn't become the way your family communicates, one day you could be looking at a moody teenager who has no idea how to share their ups and downs with you or anyone else. With every year, if a loving connection is not maintained, the ability for children to connect with you gets harder and the stakes get higher. Maintain eye contact, look friendly, express your love with a touch or a smile and keep trying.

It makes me sad to think these skills aren't being learned because kids are spending so much time focused on screens of one kind or other. Screen time replacing family time is robbing kids of the opportunity to develop strong communication and other interpersonal skills that allow them to bond and connect with others. Knowing how to comfortably relate to others is life-changing. This isn't just my opinion; the research is terrifying.

Communication skills are critical to express who we are and how we feel. We've all met adults who are not as adept at connecting with others as they could be, and I'm pretty sure you wouldn't want that life for your child. If you don't give in to the pressure your child puts on you to 'leave them alone' and insist they at least try to say something – at least that's a start.

If your child is often out of sorts or has gotten into the habit of not speaking to you, it's not going to do you any good to punish them. Here's an example of how you could engage with them, to help them open up:

> *My darling, I love you and I know you love me. I notice that when you're upset, you find it difficult to talk about it. But if we work on this together, whatever you are feeling, at least you won't be going through this alone. Believe it or not, I'm sure when you are my age you will feel exactly as I do* – hoping your child realises you love them and that you want to help them get through things. *I think you'll feel better if you do. What do you think?*

See if you can get a hug and, at the very least, try to get them to cook with you or plan something or watch telly – anything that helps them feel your love and connection. Use a loving tone and maintain eye contact when possible.

Don't worry if this feels a bit awkward in the beginning. What I want you to know is that if you can even just get them nodding at first, you will have crossed a threshold to a deeper connection just by opening up the conversation. Try open-ended statements, such as: What do you think? Let's give it a go. These are terrific because they force kids to actually think before they respond. Of course, you need to adapt everything to the child's age.

Also, ask your child questions such as: How do you think I can help you with your problem? These questions build rapport and show them they are not alone. They also enables children to see that being a part of the family is about collaborating, working together and supporting one another.

It's important to agree with any suggestions your child comes up with whenever you can, even if you have to modify them a bit when the time comes to make them happen. It's actually worth telling them that what they've suggested sounds like a good idea. If it doesn't work, let them know that 'trial and error' is sometimes how we get to the best solutions. That way they'll realise there is no point in throwing in the towel and feeling like a victim whenever something they try doesn't work out as planned.

One thing to remember is that conversation goes both ways. Parenting is not a one-way street, where you get to ask all the questions. It's important to keep two-way communication going, even if you sometimes feel like you'd rather stay in your own headspace and zone out for a while. That's one of the things about being a parent – even when we are exhausted, we still have an important job to do 24/7. That said, we also need to understand the importance of self-care. We'll get to this soon.

How to speak to children so they want to listen

Listen to what your child has to say and teaching them how to listen and respond to you are important foundation skills that not only set the tone for their competency in communication, but their self-esteem and the ease with which you all interact within the family unit.

It's important you *never plead with your children* as they'll see that as weakness and no-one respects a weak leader. You'll need to use a *confident and calm tone* of voice. Also, when learning this new skill, *don't say* things like 'would you' or 'could you' or 'please will you' when you are asking your children to do something they don't want to do. These words will make it sound as though complying with your request is optional.

When your child realises you mean what you say and they have learned to do what you ask without whining, always remember to say thank you. These two words are great at reinforcing a behaviour that we want to become a habit. If it's early days for you as a CALM Parent, remember you are in the business of behaviour modification – both your child's and your own. Behaviour modification is all about breaking unhelpful habits and forming helpful ones.

It's also important there is no confusion about who's the boss. If your child thinks they're the boss, you will need to tell them that you are taking back your proper position within the family and reassure them that all they need to do is listen and learn from you. Tell them you will give them options when you can but even if they argue and carry on about something, you will no longer be talked into changing your mind about things to do with the family.

Here are a few reminders about strategies we've discussed so far:

- Always have eye contact.
- Don't take 'I don't know' or a shrug for an answer.
- Patiently listen.
- Don't judge but guide if needed.
- Never plead.
- Use a confident, CALM tone when asking for something.
- Don't say 'would you' or 'could you' when asking for something.

Stick to your word

Sometimes the smallest things have the biggest impact when it comes to getting children to listen to you. All day long, I see parents telling their children to:

- say hello
- pick up their things
- say thank you
- take their plate to the sink
- stop a behaviour
- start a behaviour
- go to sleep
- stop whining.

Guess what? Their requests are often ignored.

Please stop saying things you don't care about or mean. Knowing when you won't be bothered to follow through is the key to getting kids to listen when you speak to them.

If it's not important to you – don't say it.

If it is important – insist until it's done.

When my youngest child, Ellie, was two, she was shy. If someone came to the front door, she would hide behind me. I would say: Ellie, say hello. Initially, she would just want to stay behind me and would ignore my request but she soon realised it was not going to be an option. I would gently pull her out from behind me, stand her next to me and ask her again to say hello. I would look into her eyes and use a tone whereby she could not mistake the request as being an option. It took only one or two times before she realised the other person was not to be feared and actually responded appreciatively to her offer of a greeting.

Let your children know what you expect of them by explaining the process and, if necessary, role-playing to help them remember. For instance, if they start arguing and carrying on about something, tell them that from now on you will ask them to stop and if they don't stop, there will be a consequence they won't like.

In addition to telling them you're not happy with their behaviour, a good incentive to discontinue what you've asked them to stop, could include confiscating their iPad (or Lego, phone or whatever they enjoy having) for a period of time – anything up to 24 hours, depending on age. While they're getting used to the idea you are taking your power back, you might want to 'count to three', to give them time to take a breath and think about what they have to do to avoid being punished by having their special things removed.

You could also think about doing a 'serious' role-play in a fun way, so your children know what to expect. It's okay to laugh and have fun while teaching your children new habits and behaviours but not at the risk of having them miss the point. To eliminate that possibility, it's a good idea to have them repeat what you've been explaining back to you to acknowledge they've understood.

Make your requests a statement rather than a question

There is no sense in using your begging voice with your child while you are retraining or asking them to do something for you. In fact, if you haven't been getting your point through to them, you will have to be slightly sterner than you would normally want to be. Once your child learns to listen and do what you need them to do, your whole family will be able to converse and communicate nicely without anyone having to be stern, angry or upset.

You might find it hard to believe right now, but if you follow the suggestions I'm making here and tailor them to your own particular situation, your family members will start communicating more and become happier and more respectful.

In the meantime, it's important you don't turn what needs to be done into a request. Make statements instead. If there is any sort of uncertainty in your voice, your child will feel like they can bargain their way out of doing what you want them to do. So if you don't use your 'don't mess with me' voice, your child will continue to try and run rings around you.

It works best if you:

- say your child's name
- ask them to look at you
- state what you want them to do
- get confirmation they have understood
- smile and walk away.

Do not hang around for a challenge.

Playing with words

Once a young child begins to comprehend what's being said to them, even at the signal-reading stage, it works to speak to their imagination. If you help open up their imagination and curiosity by asking questions, you'll find children soon begin to listen, understand and eventually learn how to think and do things for themselves. Rather than using a monotone or baby voice, try something different – perhaps the voice of a lazy lion cartoon character or a cheeky monkey.

After your child's first birthday, it's appropriate to speak to them more or less the same way you speak to anyone else you love – with kindness and a factual tone. If you keep up the baby talk, so will your child. Contrary to popular opinion, children won't get sad or offended if you speak to them 'normally'. Your child is now able to read cues from you and is old enough to realise they are still very special and loved by you, even if you use your normal voice.

I've seen parents, especially mothers, responding to out-of-control 6-year-olds with endearing words delivered in a way you would normally speak to a newborn. The problem with this is that it frustrates children and they just get madder and more abusive because their parent is walking on eggshells around them and too frightened to *take charge*. This becomes a vicious cycle where the child has the power.

The thing to be aware of is that, for the good of the family, you need to be more committed to getting your power back than the child is to holding on to it. You may have to raise your voice to be more assertive than they are so your child realises they're not going to win the battle. Or you may find a whisper will work better than turning the volume up. What definitely won't stop an out-of-control child is a tone that sounds like you are scared to step up and take control. Begin by being playful for a few seconds. If that's out of the question, don't be afraid to ramp things up while watching your child stopping in fits and spurts to observe what's going on with you – it wouldn't hurt to let out a laugh at that point. What you are trying to do is confuse them in that moment so you are able to change the neural pathway that sends them off to automatically respond in the way they have been.

If saying weird things to them or laughing doesn't work, then, if they're in a safe place, turn around and walk away. Looking bored and pretending to take interest in something else lets children know they won't get the reaction they want.

Use your imagination – or whatever it takes – to connect

Childhood can be organised, structured, playful and lots of fun if we decide to make it that way. Using your imagination and creative thinking will guide you here. Stories are a wonderful way to connect with children. I often have parents telling me they're no good at telling stories. I tell them to just start. Invariably they find they have plenty of stories up their sleeve. The earlier you start to spark your child's creativity the better. All children love listening to stories almost as much as they love making them up.

You can't raise kids without (sometimes) raising your voice

The way many parents ask their kids to do something starts off wrong and ends up even worse. The descent from wrong to worse looks and feels like being on a slippery slope as you move through the following five states:

1. Passive – Billy, can you take the plate to the sink for Mummy, please?
2. Begging – Billy, honey, would you mind taking the plate to the sink?
3. Whiney – Billy, please sweetie, do what Mummy is asking.
4. Frustrated – Billy, honestly, just take the plate. (*louder*)
5. Aggressive – Why do I have to do everything in this house? Is it really that hard to help? (*louder still and Mum takes the plate*)

I see something like the five steps above played out in stressed families all the time. There are many problems with this, not least of which is that children are being taught to expect and prime themselves for aggression – both yours and their own.

Don't despair if this scenario looks a bit like what's going on in your house. What you can do to avoid this is to remember to:

- make your request a statement rather than a question
- deliver it in a tone that leaves nothing to the imagination.

We all have automatic responses to things we hear and see. Most children's inner dialogue automatically goes straight to 'how can I get out of this?' when they are being asked to do something. Wouldn't it be easier on you, and kinder for them, to retrain them to expect they will be getting interrupted from time to time when you need them to do something? End of story.

Once kids get the message that this is how it's going to be, whenever you ask them to do something, their response will soon be a 'Yes, Mum' or 'Okay, Daddy' rather than whining or complaining.

A common variation on the 5-step slippery slope, is where things stop at step 2. In this case you decide to throw in the towel early and just do whatever you've asked them to do yourself. It's another pattern I see playing out over and over again. Whether you're on the slippery slope to step 5 or step 2, it's time to get the control back. Following are a couple of hypothetical examples to get you to start thinking about how you might go about these types of situations.

The scenario: it's time for your Billy to have a bath. Billy is engrossed in watching TV at the moment.

Method 1

You come into the room saying, "Bath time, Billy."

Billy ignores you.

"Come on darling, it's bath time. Please come now."

CHAPTER 1: COMMUNICATION

Billy makes a whiney noise then ignores you again.

You walk away because you're used to being ignored, then you come back and say, "Billy, I'm sick of doing this every single night. Please just get in the bath. You can have a quick one tonight, okay?"

Billy ignores this too.

By now, you're speaking louder and faster, verging on furious. "I'm not going to ask you again. Come now."

Now Billy is getting mad too. "Okay! I'm coming!" he shouts at you. But he just stands up and keeps staring at the TV.

"Billy! Why do we have to do this every night?" you say in an exhausted voice. Then, you start to get mad and grab him under his armpits.

Billy struggles while he gets more and more upset.

You tell him, in a very aggressive voice, how tired you are, how hard your day at work has been, and that you're at the end of your tether. You end up dumping Billy in the bath with his socks still on. You're both in tears.

The Result: Nobody is happy. And Billy probably jumped out of the bath, leaving you with yet another mess to clean up.

Method 2

You come into the room, walk over to Billy and wait a few seconds until he acknowledges your presence by looking at you. You bend down to his level, look into his eyes and in your no-nonsense voice, you say: "Billy, in two minutes I'm coming to get you for your bath. Will I turn the TV off now or will you do it then?"

Billy doesn't answer, but he does nod.

When you come back again in a few minutes, you say: "Let's go to the bath now." Your tone brooks no interference but isn't at all angry. Nothing happens, so you turn off the TV, take Billy's hand and walk him to the bathroom. While you're doing this, you're happily chatting to him about the day, keeping it light and fun. Your energy shows him you are committed to doing what you said when you first walked into the room.

Billy almost reluctantly hops in the bath, but soon starts chatting with you about his day as he listens to you telling him about what's happening on the weekend, the yummy dinner that's cooking, and how someone at work has a very naughty boy who didn't get any dinner or dessert last night.

The Result: Billy knows what to expect. He knows you are not going to put up with any complaints and he's enjoying having you to himself.

You may get a lot of resistance the first time you try your version of the second method but, before too long, you will see your commitment has made it clear to him that you mean what you say. How you get Billy in the bath is how you get him to help with anything he needs to do. Teaching responsibilities for his behaviour and how to listen to you will help him in all areas of his life.

How do you sound?

It's worth noting that when you have to reprimand the kids, it's your tone and level of commitment that will be noticed and responded to more than your words. If your child begins yelling at you, get close, look into their eyes and in your strongest, most determined and committed voice, say: Do not speak to me that way. Still in a firm voice, ask them to speak nicely and say: Then I will listen to you. If they yell again, as long as they are safe, turn and walk away. Take some deep breaths and calm down. When you're ready, come back to the child and ask them to repeat back to you what they need to do if they want something from you. Keep explaining what they need to do until they can repeat it back. Avoid terms of endearment and speak in a tone that lets them know you mean what you're saying.

Help your child to know the difference between casual chatting and being directed to do something, like getting in the bath, by the tone of voice you use. This is helping your child to understand what leadership looks like and will stand them in good stead when it is time for them to step up and be assertive themselves. Not only are you getting things done without drama but you are also teaching important life skills to your children.

The art of communication for you in this space is about perfecting a tone in which your children know what you are saying is non-negotiable. If you have been in the habit of using a baby tone, with words like 'bubby', 'sweetie' or 'buddy', to get your children to do things they don't want to do, you will find this new way of communicating will make things a whole lot easier for everyone.

We all hope our children will grow up able to make logical decisions. We love to encourage their ability to do this by asking them what, when or how they would like things in their life to happen. However, you always know best. You can help your children with decision-making and communication skills at family meetings when you encourage collaborative decision making about how their week will go. We discuss this further in the management chapter.

As I wind this chapter up, I want to impress upon you the importance of always engaging with your child by:

- using eye contact
- ensuring your words mean something
- never letting them ignore you or what you say
- refraining from repeating yourself if you are not getting through
- saying things in a different way
- noticing what your tone is saying.

Don't worry if it feels like I'm asking you to climb a mountain here. The other chapters in this book are about helping you to build your confidence in the realm of parenting. As your confidence builds, so will your communication skills and vice versa.

CHAPTER 2: ATTENTION

When you pay attention to detail, the big picture will take care of itself.
— Georges St-Pierre

Now we're ready to move beyond autopilot and stop to have a look at what's really going on around and within you. Above all, this is the time to become more aware of yourself and the other members of the family. This is important, because it's only when you are on top of your own game you'll notice and effectively attend to the needs of others.

It takes a village

Most parents I know are doing their best; we can only do things in relation to what we know, right? And we don't know what we don't know, so there's no point beating yourself up for not getting things right all the time. I bring this point up because I see so many parents, mums in particular, who bitterly defend themselves against anyone trying to give advice in regard to their parenting.

Unfortunately, I was the mum who had blinkers on whenever anyone tried to help me see how I could be making things easier for myself and my first-born. On some level, I knew I was giving in far too much but I was committed to some crazy notion I was being a selfless, loving mum.

In the back of my mind, I was also thinking my daughter was learning to be a strong woman. I didn't want to make her feel anything less than amazing all the time but I never considered what happened at day care, or any other time she wasn't with me. For example, on Vanessa's second time at day care, the teachers wanted to see me. They said that Vanessa took her shoes off as asked but then stood at the front of the room and told the other children, in her biggest voice, to take their shoes off and put them along the wall. I found this admirable. They didn't.

On some level, we all tend to defend what isn't working in our lives. I have found this to be the case with parents I've met. Whenever anyone points out that their parenting could work better if they tried this or that, most would say something like: Excuse me. This is how we do it. Essentially, parents feel they are being told that what they're doing isn't working. Deep down, all parents are afraid they're failing or could be doing better – but isn't that true, in all areas of life, when we're learning a new skill or in a new job? For some reason, we all think that parenting should be natural for us to know what to do and that's why we become defensive.

With all the uncertainty that comes with the first child and the exhaustion that comes with lack of sleep or having more than one little person to deal with, the last thing we want is advice from someone who 'sees' what is really going on and, even if they craft it in the most delicate way, it's clear to us they think we could be doing better.

I feel quite sad when I see parents who are really struggling but are too proud to ask for help and end up turning to social media for confirmation they are doing okay. On the other side of the coin, it's also sad when well-meaning people, such as mothers-in-law or grandparents, notice the frustration and struggles their loved ones are having but are too afraid to say anything – they feel it's none of their business. However, isn't that what grandparents are for – to give support and love?

> *We all need help when it comes to parenting because it does take a village to raise a child.*

I'd love to see a lot more honest communication around parenting, where everyone is brave enough to say what needs to be said without the fear of having their head bitten off. Authentic and loving communication is far more helpful than misplaced diplomacy where people feel the need to bite their tongue or just say what they think you want to hear. I prefer my friends and family to be honest and tell me anything they think will help me, even if my feelings get hurt a little. Why? The obvious answers are usually right in front of us but often we just don't see it until it's too late to do anything.

Make manners matter – notice what's going on

I've worked with many families who have children who refuse to say please or thank you. I've also worked with a couple of families whose children had difficulty pronouncing certain words. You might be wondering how these two things are connected? The solution to both problems is actually the same. First, we have to notice. Then, we need to help our child create a new habit by showing them what to do and remind them until they get it. As parents, sometimes it takes extra time and effort to turn things around.

I'm really passionate about this because helping children to correct 'behavioural' problems makes a huge difference to the way their lives pan out. You might be thinking that a speech difficulty isn't a behavioural problem. While we could split hairs or debate about what to call it, all that matters is that new habits can be formed with enough attention.

I have corrected more than one stutterer, thumb sucker and nail biter. It wasn't an overnight process and it wasn't easy – it required persistence. To some extent, your success depends on how much time you spend teaching your child how to change. For instance, if a child can't say the letter 's' correctly, teach them where their tongue goes, what their teeth do and what shape the lips make. Think up sentences with the letter 's' in them and turn the whole thing into a game.

Children actually respond really well to this type of instruction because they enjoy the one-on-one time with you, especially if you manage to make it fun. I would sit kids at the bench while I prepared vegetables for dinner, or I'd encourage them to help me fold the washing while we practised saying crazy things like silly slithery snakes start screaming something shocking when you stand on them.

Going back to 'please' and 'thank you' – teaching this can be turned into a fun experience. If you hand you child something and they don't say thank you, hold on to the object with a firm grip. There might be a little bit of tug-of-war but, invariably, the child 'remembers' to say thank you. Similarly, if I get a request without a please, I pretend I didn't hear it. I do this in a fun way but I still get the point across because, by about the third time, the child 'remembers' to say the 'magic words' and it soon becomes a new habit.

What should families focus on?

A happy family life is one that focuses on the family, their wellbeing and fun times together. This way, everyone feels appreciated while also appreciating each other. Living this way we can then begin to see how our words and actions affect others in the family.

It's important for children to know you are not only their parent but, just like them, you are a person who has a life that matters. Kids need to know it's not all about them.

You also have things you love to do as well as other things you don't really like doing very much but have to do. When children observe your 'can do' attitude they will learn that, just like them, you want to have a life worth living as well as being their mum or dad.

Many families operate with the children as the main focus. In these families, every decision is made to satisfy a child's wants or needs before anything else. I've seen this time and time again. While acknowledging your children's feelings is important, it doesn't mean you have to be a slave to their every whim. Children naturally become entitled if parents show their child that they are all that matters.

All kids need to learn that considering others and pulling their weight is how they're going to be able to get on happily in the family and society as a whole. Overindulged children are only happy when the world is revolving around them. Parents who are self-sacrificing and consistently putting the child's needs before their own, will soon realise they are creating a burden for themselves and for the child. The rest of the world is not going to bend over backwards to satisfy their insatiable wants and needs.

Essentially, you are setting your children up to fail if you're not training them to be considerate of the needs of others. Children need to be taught the skills needed to get by and thrive in this world. Helping children feel their feelings and understand that others also have feelings will stand them in good stead and allow them to grow up to be grounded and confident adults.

Be aware of being manipulated

I'm not saying to ignore your kids' feelings or to toughen them up or anything like that. In fact, the last thing you want to do is give children the sense their feelings aren't important. Denying feelings is a certain pathway to future problems. That said, overindulged children will often conjure up fake emotions, including misery, to manipulate their parents into giving in to them. If parents don't give in, the child who is used to always getting their way is likely to stage an Academy Award-winning performance of anger, sulking and whining until you cave in. Do your children a favour by helping them realise that being moody is not an option if they want to have a happy family life. Children must learn how to feel and process their feelings, rather than repressing them and acting out as a way of managing them.

Helping your children learn how to first deal with what's upsetting them, and then move on so they can snap out of a bad mood is a great habit to teach them. It's so much better than catering to their every whim. Our job as parents is to help our kids understand *everyone* in the family has needs just as important as theirs. That's why we have one leader, or a leadership team of mum and dad, who see the bigger picture and decide how the family will work. The fact is that parents see and know things kids simply don't. If you fall into the trap of opening every decision up for discussion, then you will be spending way too much of your precious time explaining yourself to demanding children who, deep down, really just need certainty and to be told what they need to do.

Personally, I would rather spend my time enjoying my family in the knowledge that children will bounce in and out of moods all of the time. The point I really want to drive home here is that it's not your obligation to give in to get your kids to love you more or stop being moody. Helping everyone stay on track and be grateful for what they have and creating strong bonds and more love – this is your leadership role. Sticking to this will help your kids build up all the emotional and practical resources they need to have a fulfilling life. Don't forget – children are smart. They can always see what's going on. But you are smarter.

Sharing stories to encourage feelings

It's great to share stories and engage children in what's happened in your day when you're encouraging them to share their day. It's valuable for children to understand what your life involves on a daily basis and show them you also have a million things to do every day. Sharing your stories not only helps children have empathy for you but also helps them put the things going on in their own lives into perspective. Filling your children in on the good and bad things that might be going on, keeping it age appropriate of course, will give them an understanding of the fact you have a busy life away from them. Among other things, you will show them how you manage to bounce back when things don't go to plan. Seeing you do this will help them build confidence around their ability to handle their own feelings and set-backs when they arise.

Discussing feelings helps us acknowledge them, stay in touch with them and know that even the toughest feelings will pass eventually. If tough feelings persist, children who are secure about their place within the family will know there will always be someone around to talk to about what's going on and a helping hand whenever they need it.

Needless to say, the art of really connecting and sharing life's ups and downs with others entails a preparedness to be vulnerable. Don't get caught in the trap of thinking that vulnerability equals weakness. The opposite is actually true. Among other things, creating an environment at home where people feel comfortable enough to show their vulnerability to each other is probably one of the best things you could possibly do for your children and yourself.

The reality of the busy lives so many of us lead means we must be vigilant when it comes to maintaining enough awareness to notice when the moments of connection within the family are petering out. There's a lot at stake here. Feeling understood and having a deep sense of belonging is a legacy your children will thrive on if you put in the work to create solid foundations and maintain a level of attention where you know what's actually going on.

Let's face it, parenting can feel like a selfless chore a lot of the time. Helping your children see you for the person you really are – their superhero – means they will be in a better position to appreciate that, even if they don't like something you're suggesting, they should still do what you say, because you deserve that respect.

CHAPTER 3: LEADING

A leader is one who knows the way, goes the way, and shows the way.
— John C Maxwell

In raising future adults, you must make your decisions with an eye to the bigger picture. If you're just trying to keep your child happy for now, I want to ask you: when will you help them learn how to become self-aware and capable of dealing with the things that life is going to throw at them? If your child is constantly disrespecting you and others, this pattern of behaviour has been created because you've allowed it to happen. I don't say this to put the blame on you but because now is the time to acknowledge what's really going on. Once you decide to change things, you will be giving your child the foundations they need to have a happy life. So, let's face the facts about what hasn't been working and then we can move on to embrace the solutions.

What I learned at day care

I'll never forget the shock I felt on the first day I dropped my 2-and-a-half-year-old off at day care for the very first

CHAPTER 3: LEADING

time. As I said, my first child, Vanessa, was born very clever and very strong-willed and I loved that in her. In fact, I actually named her after Vanessa Redgrave, the epitome, to me, of a woman with strength.

What an eye-opener that first day was. I dropped Vanessa off, then went back to get her about half an hour later. I guess I didn't quite have my head around the idea of leaving her with strangers the first time. Once I got my nerve back, I dropped her off again but stayed for an hour to see if the people running the centre were capable of dealing with my child's 'special' personality.

While I was at the centre, I noticed there were some other strong-willed children who were the loudest and the busiest. They'd actually been given responsibility for organising some of the kids' playgroups. I remember wondering how my 'special' child was going to deal with that. By 'that', I mean 'them'. My sense was she wasn't going to like it.

I was actually wrong. Amazingly, Vanessa settled in quite well. It was me who had some growing up to do. In fact, I had a couple of key realisations on that day. The first one was I hadn't really taught Vanessa how to deal with other strong-willed children. Fortunately, she worked it out for herself. The second insight was that children love structure. This dawned on me as I watched the way the head teacher masterfully handled morning tea time. First she told everyone who would like a piece of fruit to stand up. I noticed her tone was firm – quite firm. She then started counting heads. As she did that, those who hadn't already stood up seemed to automatically stand up. It was like magic. She stood them in a row and touched them on the head as she enthusiastically said their name and sent them to the table to eat. There was no kerfuffle. The children just fell into line and did as they were told. This was a revelation to me.

Essentially, the head teacher was acting like a leader. As the leader, she had established the day's structure for the children and they all knew what was expected of them. That was the day I got to see just how much kids respect a leader, and love structure. I really took on board what I saw on that first day and before too long, Vanessa got to see what it was like to have a mother who was starting to dip her toe into the business of acting like a leader.

One of the main principles I noticed that day was when you ask kids to do something, you have to sound like you mean it. You also have to help them appreciate it's in their interest to comply and you need to say their name to make them feel acknowledged. Don't be wishy-washy. Just get on with it.

Everyone wants to be boss

It's important for everyone to know who's the boss because if *you* don't lead your family, you will find your children will more than happily lead you. As cute as it might seem the first few times your adorable little munchkin acts like Margaret Thatcher, I promise it will soon wear thin if you are constantly being challenged on every decision you make and on every single thing you ask your children to do.

Here are the four principles you need to start thinking about if you want to be seen as the leader.

- Always think of yourself as the leader of your family.
- Act like a leader by never accepting disrespect.
- Speak with authority when you need to.
- Notice what's not working and take action to rectify it ASAP.

This may sound simple enough but if you've been winging it for years, grinning and bearing the chaos that has ensued, you're going to have to brace yourself against the weight of inertia and pushback from the children to start your leadership inhouse training. Take time to prepare yourself and acknowledge the time has come to put more balance and control in your life.

Up until now, it's probably been a case of giving your all to a job outside the home, then getting home exhausted, only to find there's still plenty of things to do before you can turn in for the night. There's the washing, cooking, cleaning up, responding to emails, putting kids in the bath, helping them with their homework, brushing teeth, reading stories before putting them to bed and any number of other things it takes to run a home.

Part of your new role as a leader is to have your kids *help* you get the practical things around the house done on a daily basis. The problem for most parents who call me in to help them get back control of their life is they've fallen into the habit of begging their kids, adopting a tone of voice that makes it sound as if they're in some kind of trouble or putting on a fake sweet voice – all in the hope of getting a little assistance with the daily workload.

The sad thing is that most of the time parents feel as though there is no other way. They keep on nagging, cajoling and repeating requests for help, day after day. It's like a broken record of 'clean your room, make your bed, get off the iPad, get into the shower, answer me when I speak to you, empty the dishwasher ...' It's exhausting. In the end, most parents give up, shut up and say nothing while they do it all themselves.

Parents who've reached burnout often default to this option because they think it's just easier that way.

It is absolutely not easier.

In actual fact, it's not even nicer.

What you may need is to take the time to help your children understand the importance of assisting with family chores and becoming an *active* participant in the running of your home. You might be surprised how much their confidence and moods begin to change for the better when they see how important they actually are in the scheme of things. When children really slot into their role as an important member of the family team and start to push themselves a little to accomplish things, no matter how small those things are, they get to experience feelings of true self-worth.

With the right attitude underlying your directions, children actually love to help because they want to be able to do things just like you do. For this to happen, you need to reinforce good behaviour by praising them when they've done their best to help. For some of the families I've worked with, it's hard for parents to imagine what it's like to have children who clean up after themselves and consistently try to do the right thing without having to be asked all the time. I love helping parents see that bringing control and cooperation into their family doesn't have to be complicated. All it takes is for them to make the decision to step up and act like a leader who's on top of things. This is important because families work much better when there is a clearly defined hierarchy in place.

There needs to be no doubt in anyone's mind that you and your partner, if relevant, are the leaders of the team and that you have responsibility for making the decisions. While you're getting used to this, it's worth telling yourself daily that you're a loving leader. Leadership is not about becoming a heartless authoritarian. It's about lovingly creating an environment where respect and growth can form the foundation for everything that goes on in the home. A loving leader makes life easy for the other team members, by helping them know exactly what they need to do to play their part. It's important you are not wishy-washy about your position as the leader because any weakness in your resolve will water down your authenticity and may result in pushback – leading to constant pressure from children making it hard for you to be your best loving self.

Beginning to eliminate what's not working

Don't panic if you feel like you're in a bit of a mess right now. Try to make constructive changes one at a time and don't hesitate to get some help if you need it. You don't have to go it alone. You also don't have to try to fix everything all at once. I recommend you start by eliminating any problems you have allowed to develop because of a misplaced belief they will benefit your child, such as catering to laziness and allowing children to challenge you. Once you've identified these things, firmly tell the kids you're not going to be pandering to them anymore. You can say this without it sounding aggressive – use a calm 'I mean it' voice to let them know things are going to be changing and from now on there is going to be a lot more structure around their days. That's where it all has to start.

The underlying principle is that parenting should not be about suffering. However, there's no getting away from the fact that leaders of the home and the family have a lot to do. Managing your time effectively and delegating tasks where appropriate, as well as eliminating time-wasters, such as needing everything to be perfect, are all strategies you should adopt sooner rather than later. These strategies will help you create a home everyone enjoys being a part of.

How to restore and rebuild connections

There is nothing more important to humans than to have deep and meaningful connections. Bonding and feeling valued by others, especially those we love, helps us feel safe in the world and gives us certainty. Most children today are overreacting to the smallest of things because no matter how many times you say 'I love you, you're amazing', more often than not, they're just not feeling it. I believe it's because children have quite often lost respect for their parents, seeing them as easy to manipulate and weak in their decision-making.

Children who are bossing their parents around have a warped sense of their role in the family and who the leader is. The connection isn't healthy for either party, neither is it sustainable. Sooner or later, the parent will have to stand up for themselves and that's when the challenged child feels hurt and unfairly treated. The connection begins to form a chink in the armour. The child begins to think of the parent as the enemy – you against me.

Sadly, I see this kind of thing in more families each year.

Every time the child loses his position of 'boss', he begins to feel angry, uncertain, unimportant and disconnected – to name just a few things he may be going through. Your child has become addicted to the buzz of bossing you around, as well as the fun of the challenge.

Avoiding this scenario is easy.

Begin with having compassion for you and your child. I remember my first child trying to boss me around and how cute I thought that was. If I were completely honest, I also knew it wasn't going to end well so I began justifying my inability to stop her as her opportunity to gain confidence, learn how to negotiate and become self-assured.

Anyone else been there?

Manipulation, co-dependency and addiction are the three things children learn.

Once children see themselves as your boss, they are not going to hand that title over to you or give up that behaviour happily without a fight. If this is you, and you need things to change, you are going to have to be prepared for a whole heap of backlash and loud complaints before reality sets in.

Here's what needs to happen:

1. Have a family meeting – explain how things need to change, it's all your fault and that you can see that they are crying a whole lot more than they should be. Tell them you will take back your parenting role and they need to just relax and be happy as the child. Let them know you will allow them to make decisions occasionally and that you will be clear when that's an option.

2. Role-play what will happen from now on – that can be lots of fun and very engaging. You will say their name and *they will look at you*; you will tell them what you need them to do and *they will respond while looking at you*; then, straight away, *they will do what you ask*. Role-play these three things and HAVE FUN DOING IT.

3. You will explain there will be consequences if they do not listen and learn or do what you ask. Role-play that. Be reasonable for the first week and make the consequences light but if they are not trying to change then the consequences will need to be tougher until they realise the rules have changed and they need to as well.

It's important for a child's development to know where they stand in the family so they can behave accordingly. When it is clear you are the leader and they are here to listen to you and learn from you, then the child can relax and play – letting you make the decisions. When this is not clear and the respect for you is lost, how can the child feel confident when you praise them, or trust you are an authority on anything? It's very difficult for them to feel confident you know what you are doing if you keep changing your mind when pressure is put on you. Even their love can become more of an unhealthy co-dependency because without you there giving in to them, no-one else understands, so they often become clingy.

Our parenting has to always consider the bigger picture and our parenting job has to entail helping our children become well-balanced adults with an ability to listen to and respect others so they can be constantly on a journey of learning and growth. Life doesn't always cater to us or give us what we want but without pushing ourselves and giving a little effort in the way I am describing here to you, then our children will not reach their full potential and may not cope in the outside world.

Respect

Establishing yourself as a leader is not about ego. It's about giving your child someone they can trust and rely on, someone to look up to and be guided by. No-one wants to follow a leader who keeps changing their mind or gives in all the time. You can be the leader your children need you to be. This means being confident about telling them what they have to do and what they need to know, while reassuring them all they need is to listen with an open heart and do what is expected of them.

There are two things I consider to be the bedrock of healthy families. Respect is one of them and trust is the other. You will read more about trust in Chapter 5.

I often see parents falling into the trap of wanting to be liked over wanting to be respected. There's nothing wrong with your children liking you but without respect, your bond will slowly diminish. If you're in the habit of allowing your child to feel superior to you, it has to stop. Your child needs to believe you are amazing and look up to you with unconditional positive regard because you are the mum and dad – and now you are teaching your child how to be an amazing adult, too.

Establishing a home where trust and respect are a given relies on your ability to be clear in your communication and consistent in your behaviour. I want you to worry a lot less about being the 'cool' parent and about your child not liking you. I want you to care *more* about giving your children self-confidence, direction and self-awareness.

I don't like saying this, but after years of working in this space, I know without a doubt that leaders need to be prepared 'to be cruel to be kind'. Rest assured, even if your kids think you're being tough on them, they will still love you as well as respect you – even if they act differently at first.

The fact is that children love having a good leader to follow. Look at how they adore their sports coaches, piano teacher, band leaders etc. Even the harshest ballet teachers are adored. These people do not pander to children's whims. They push them to do their best and so should you. Your children will respect you for this. Children want to feel that their parents know what is good for them and their development. Children are looking for a leader they can trust to always be there, helping them to grow and learn.

Two things to focus on to get children to respect you

To put it simply, to earn respect, you need to do two things:

Remove guilty parenting and stay strong in your resolve

We all have times as a parent when we know we could have done better. Maybe we could have given better advice, or been more patient, or stricter, or more present. Maybe we could have asked more questions, taken more time or been more honest. Well, guess what? That's okay. Who cares? For starters, you've done your best and what's more, if necessary, you can always apologise and admit you've done something wrong at any time. Don't hesitate to admit you're not perfect. This is a great thing to do when the time is right because you're teaching your children all the time and they will be able to model you getting over mistakes without being a drama queen. There will be times when it would be best not to muddy the waters by drawing attention to the fact you made a mistake – obviously you need to use your judgement here.

What you don't want to do is ruminate over the mistakes you've made and spend time feeling guilty. A guilty parent sometimes compounds their pain by overcompensating and giving in when they are being challenged, purely because they are feeling guilty. If you find yourself resorting to these kinds of unhelpful behaviours, you just need to notice what's really going on and cut yourself some slack. Just like you're teaching your children to do, you are also breaking out of old habits that no longer serve you.

Establish the rules

You need to have a clear set of rules on which to develop and maintain boundaries. This will give children a solid foundation where they know what they can and cannot do. What you're likely to find is that identifying the rules is not particularly tricky, however, getting your kids to always respect the rules at first can be. You might like to help your children understand what the rules are by talking about them at your weekly family meetings.

You'll be hearing about family meetings in the next chapter. Essentially, though, in family meetings, you can link the rules to things that have happened during the previous week, as well as looking at what's happening in the upcoming week and what they will need to do.

The name of the game is making it very clear to the children *exactly* what you expect from them. You can make sure they understand by getting them to paraphrase what you've just said. If you like, you can even do a bit of a role-play to make it a bit more fun. By making the family meetings a fun experience, where you continually reinforce the rules one way or another, you'll be surprised to find that your children will not only really enjoy the meetings but with a bit of luck, they'll also start respecting rules without even noticing they are doing it.

Don't be surprised if there is some resistance to change among the younger members of the family, especially in the case of banning unhelpful behaviours that have previously become a habit. What you need to do here is keep your vision for your family in mind and let that guide your responses to any complaints from your children that you have to handle. This brings me back to the point I made earlier – let go of wanting your child's approval. Every person who experienced life with parents who were firm and loving will tell you they had a great childhood.

Wouldn't it be nice if you didn't have to waste time doing and saying the same things a million times a day? It may take a few weeks or even months of extra effort from you and your children to get to that point but I guarantee that once your position as a leader has been established, and you've put rules and firm boundaries in place that are understood by your children, you'll be happily surprised to see how well they respond to you with more respect, love and admiration.

The attitude you adopt when you're teaching kids how to help with particular tasks is important. You're trying to get them on board rather than continually having to make them do their chores. Forcing them is likely to generate resentment, and resentment will only lead to a bad job being done as well as a child who needs to be reminded every time. If you notice an attitude like resentment welling up, just pull the child aside and talk about what's going on. Depending on how they react to being called to task, you could ask them if they would feel loved if you were grumpy and sulky every time you did something for them.

When you ask your children to do something, your voice needs to become a little bit slower and louder than usual, but without emotion. Your tone needs to tell them it is not negotiable but, at the same time, it shouldn't sound like it's a punishment. It's best to start by giving your children small tasks to do every day, so they will get into the habit of helping. For example, let the kids grab the groceries off the shelf to put in the trolley and then have them help you put them away when you get home.

From the age of about 7, children can be shown how to put a load of washing on and fold it when it's dry. Even a 2-year-old can hand you pegs while you put washing on the line. Don't ever fall for the idea that getting children to help around the house is child abuse. It is actually quite the opposite. They are learning a valuable life skill – one day they will be running a household of their own and won't even blink an eye, let alone moan about it, like so many do.

The take-home message from this chapter is that great leaders don't happen by accident.

CHAPTER 4: MANAGING

Management is doing things right. Leadership is doing the right things.
— Peter Drucker

Managing a home and family can be overwhelming, especially when you're also managing a career, looking after aging parents, dealing with financial stress or any number of other things that can leave us with very little fuel in the tank to focus on our own wellbeing. Taking time to regularly rejuvenate and reset and being conscious of *your* needs will set you up to be a better parent.

Let me ask you this: Do you need to change your thinking to allow yourself space for self-care? I might not have all the answers for you but what I want to do in this chapter is really get you thinking about finding the time for yourself so you can effectively manage everyone and everything else it takes to run a family.

Sometimes, being a parent makes us feel like we need to be superhuman just to get through everything we are responsible for. There's so much to think about and do that it's easy to get overwhelmed and start feeling like it's impossible to get everything done.

Managing feelings

Every now and then, it's worth reminding your children it's okay to feel things like overwhelm and exhaustion. The fact is, everyone experiences 'unpleasant' feelings as well as good ones. It's okay to feel sad and confused sometimes as well. It's all part of the human experience.

We shouldn't feel we have to hide our feelings from our children because, essentially, we are the guiding light showing them how important it is to be real with each other. Living an authentic life together, feeling our feelings without shame or fear of being judged and always remembering we are loved makes us strong.

Of course, nobody wants to burden children with complaints all the time or with having a complete meltdown. Just use your common sense about what's appropriate for children of their age to see but don't act as if you can always handle everything without even the occasional hiccup.

Looking for solutions rather than dwelling on problems is the key here and it's a good life skill to teach. Authentic parenting helps children know things don't always happen as we want them to but because we're all in this together, we'll always be okay.

Managing changes

Changes sometimes occur when we're not expecting them, and sometimes expected changes don't happen. Once again, this is an opportunity to teach your children strong life skills – acceptance and flexibility in this case. No matter what life may bring our way, it's good to embrace what we feel, then remember those feelings will always pass and make way for new feelings to emerge. It's good to let children know that no feeling will ever be more than they can handle because we are always there to help each other through.

That's why it's better to acknowledge that they *feel* sad, rather than saying that children *are* sad. Similarly, rather than saying that Billy *is* bad, it's better to say Billy *is behaving badly*. Always reminding our children they are perfect little adults in training and that we are the trainers, helps our children get things into perspective and lets them know we are all learning and we, too, have trainers.

You want your children to know that it's safe to express how they are feeling within the family and that they need never feel alone because they are part of a loving family who are always there, learning and growing together to support each other.

As adults we know that everyone's life does not necessarily match their Facebook profiles. In fact, no-one on the planet manages to completely avoid *all* challenges and difficulties. Coming up against hard times now and then is just another part of life. And, just like the good times, they will come and go. Life is like a merry-go-round, so don't push feelings away – feel them, let them pass and move on.

Teaching children about the range of emotions they may experience, such as curiosity, compassion, disgust, shame, anxiety or conceit to name a few, helps them to understand it's not all just good and bad. It can even be fun trying to describe how you feel or how they do. You can then practise sitting with the feeling silently for a moment and then move on. Even when we have the most urgent, painful or upsetting feelings, it's possible to ride the wave for just a few minutes, then watch it fade away out into the distance. What a great life lesson you are teaching. Of course, some feelings last longer but my belief is that our mind can give us the feeling and it can also take it away.

Long-term problems are the result of people pushing negative feelings down. Basically, never facing our fears is setting us up for trouble. When we face our fears, we get to experience the fact that once we've dealt with our feelings they can no longer run our life or define us. A great attitude to adopt is that even if something only happened yesterday, it was in the past and it's gone. The problem is that not feeling our feelings leaves that energy to build up inside our bodies. At first you might not even notice it. It might just be a niggling feeling of being unsettled, especially when it's being triggered by a familiar event. But if you keep pushing your feelings down for too long, they are going to come out one way or another. Learning how to feel it and move it along with some positive support is a great way to teach kids and try it for ourselves.

Helping our children learn how to deal with things is an important parenting job, as is ensuring communication lines are always open. That way, our children can feel comfortable telling us anything. I would always tell my children: I don't care what happens. Even if whatever has gone on is your fault, I will always be by your side. They've never forgotten that.

As adults, they often bring this up when we're reminiscing about the good old days. It was a good thing I had that attitude too because they often told me things I wished I didn't have to hear. But no matter what, together we always got through whatever was going on at any given time. We came out of it usually relatively unscathed and always stronger.

Managing difficult conversations

What I'm about to say now might sound a bit odd but the fact is that I like difficult conversations. I honestly believe they are the ones that make us into the people we need to become to craft out the life we want to be living. Most people try to avoid difficult conversations because they are afraid of confrontation or they don't want to create an outcome they may not like. Isn't it better to try to facilitate an outcome that suits us rather than walking on eggshells, worrying about what might happen?

It makes no sense, when you think about it, to render ourselves powerless or spend needless time worrying just to avoid feeling a little bit uncomfortable about having a difficult conversation. If things need to change, they need to change. It's okay. Nothing stays the same anyway – not in nature, nor in humans. The sooner we accept that fact, the sooner we can relax and learn to accept the things we can't do anything about.

That said, many people find change more difficult than it needs to be. If you're one of those people, don't feel bad – you're not alone. From firsthand experience, I've learned that learning to embrace change helps you begin to build up your confidence and you might actually begin to enjoy it.

Managing your position as role model

To begin with a difficult conversation about change and parenting, I want you to ask yourself if you've noticed any of your behaviours or comments that are not helping you achieve the relationships and family dynamics you want.

Take a moment to *slow down* and think back a little. What makes you happy about your family? What doesn't? What can you do if you need changes? Often, something as simple as taking a walk or meditating can help you become clear on this and when you return it may not seem as drastic as you first thought.

Once you know where you need to make changes, you're already halfway there. One thing I want you to consider before you begin changing the way you parent is whether you need to change a few things, including how you feel about yourself and your wellbeing.

There are many supportive resources available online that you might want to take a look at if you need help to feel more in control of your emotions and reactions. I'm not going to go into these in much detail here, but I do recommend that you identify things you like to do and find ways to do them more.

By doing this, you will have a life outside of the family as well as inside it. Maybe you could sign up for a short course or find a special interest group you want to join. Or perhaps you'd like to just hang out in nature. The important thing is to do things that make you feel good – and do them on a regular basis.

Teach yourself to *slow down* and take more time to think and review rather than just staying on auto – like I did. When you know you are making better decisions because you took the time to evaluate, you'll be more confident and an inspiring role model.

Managing discipline

Discipline seems to have become something of a dirty word. I almost hesitate to use the word for fear of being howled down, but I believe most people don't fully understand what discipline is. Many people think of discipline as punishment used to prevent disobedience. In that context, it does sound somewhat harsh. However, discipline actually comes from a Latin word, meaning 'instruction' and 'knowledge'.

So what is discipline really? It's about teaching. What I want to make sure is you learn to slow down and get more balance in your life.

As a parent, once we have addressed self-discipline, we must move on to exercising discipline as a parent. Discipline is necessary to teach children the rules of the world, beginning with the rules of the family.

It's about giving children boundaries and guidelines to live by. It's about exploring what those boundaries are and explaining helpful ways for children to adhere to them. When they understand the reasons for needing to stick to them, you'll find your children are much more likely to come along for the ride.

As far as I'm concerned, things like rules, training and education are gifts we give to our children. Believe it or not, they feel safer and less anxious living within the limits you set for them.

One of the key concepts I've come to understand as a mother and Nanny, is children need and, in fact, love rules. They want to know where they stand. They want stability, structure and regularity. That doesn't mean they have to live in a square box and never do anything that's fun. Far from it.

The point I'm making is that without rules, children will feel confused and ungrounded. That state can easily turn into out-of-control behaviour, if they don't know where they stand and they don't feel certain that what you say goes, every time. Inevitably, they will push the moving boundaries to see how far they can go. That's why they will beg, whine, hit, yell or argue at every opportunity. If it's worked before, why wouldn't it work this time?

One day they're allowed to have ice cream. The next day they're not. If your children are used to negotiating and often getting their own way, then why would they stop? They would find it very confusing if they begged and screamed last time until they got what they wanted, but this time they asked nicely and didn't get it. Naturally, they conclude that maybe they need to scream louder this time, to get the ice cream they so desperately want.

Take another example: One day you're on the phone and the children begin making annoying sounds. You tell them to stop', which they do for a second. When they start up again, and you give up telling them to stop, they conclude that not really caring what you want must be okay. It might not seem like such a big deal but it is actually ground-breaking. At what point will 'no' start meaning 'no' to you and your children?

One of the consequences is likely to be that when you tell them to 'stop' in future, they won't think twice about continuing because they've come to understand you don't really mean what you say anyway. Unfortunately that's the kind of rod you're making for your own back when you don't teach your children discipline and respect for you as their parent. In other words, if we don't teach our children what the boundaries are in terms of the behaviour we expect from them, they are likely to develop negative behaviours and get into trouble, be confused and feel misunderstood. Once again, it is not their fault.

The lesson here is not to let your children put pressure on you when they hear a 'no' or get disappointed. Stop their out-of-control behaviour and help them by teaching them self-control and sticking to your word. Stop your child overreacting and carrying on if they don't get their own way. It's just annoying and creates disharmony in your home or while you're out and about doing things.

Once you have the behaviour you want from your child, acknowledge it in a really positive and grateful tone, then return to being your normal self. Do not hold resentment or anger. Don't be moody. Instead, practise bouncing back and make sure being 'happy' is your family's natural state.

Managing self-control and consequences

What I want you to do is notice when you are being ignored. The next time this happens, you should give a short direct instruction. For example, if you are on the phone and the noise from the children goes up a decibel or two, immediately take charge. Put the phone down and go over to the children, look them in the eye and say: Stop making noise; what did I just say? It's worth getting them to say it back to you, so you have an 'agreement'. If your tone is controlled and determined, you will find the children listen.

If your children haven't listened to you and continue making noise, you will need to apply consequences. To reinforce the fact you mean business, the consequence could involve sending them off to do something for you – perhaps peeling the potatoes, cleaning the bath or tidying the shoe cupboard. Find a chore they can begin to do without you. If it is something they're not particularly going to like, they will get to understand the association between not doing the right thing and having to do something that is somewhat unpleasant. Your next step is to go back and finish your call. Once you're off the phone, tell the children to let you know when they finish the jobs you've allocated to them so you can inspect the results.

If they are very little children (5 or under), you may need to show them how to do the task properly when you are doing the inspection. As long as they've given it their best shot, you can show them how to do it in a fun way – like singing a silly song as you work. Once you're finished, sit down with your children and let them know that from now on, you will be removing all their treats and giving them all of your jobs if they don't do what you ask. Then say: Do you understand? Getting a yes from them is good and getting them to repeat it back to you is even better. Also don't allow attitude while you are teaching your children how to have self-control.

You might think it's more work, and not easy to do, because:

- they won't comply
- the treatment is a bit harsh
- they'll just make a mess so you're better off doing it yourself.

The point of this exercise is much bigger than 'excuses' or taking the 'easy' way out – it's far more important than that. It's about teaching your children that things are changing and from now on you are expecting them to listen to you and do as they are told. Once you've shown them the things you want them to do, you need to hold your ground. Giving in will water down your ability to maintain your position as the leader.

It's not unusual for me to be called into families where the children think the rules don't apply to them. They think this way because they've been given the impression the world revolves around them. But that's not actually how the world works and, on some level, the parents who reach out for help know they are actually setting their children up for failure if they don't find a way to turn things around.

Most people I speak to about disciplining their children tell me they don't want to be a tyrant. They don't want their child not to love them. The paradox is that children want and need to be given instructions on how to be well-behaved and helpful. It could save a lot of angst and time if new parents got this advice up front because it's actually much harder to break bad habits later than it is to establish good ones from the beginning.

I don't want you to throw the baby out with the bathwater. Nor do I want to give the impression it's too hard to get children to change. I do, however, want you to push through the transition period and on to the light at the end of the tunnel.

The important thing is to understand that commitment and consistency are key qualities needed to make change happen. You'll need to be persistent, determined and happily positive while explaining what's going on. Your children are forming new neural pathways in their little heads. That's what's actually going on when you're trying to get them to change their behaviour and at first it's like going against the natural flow of things for them.

Children are like energetic little sponges. Among other things, this means they are absorbing everything they see you do and everything they hear you say. It's our own well-intentioned but misguided parenting methods that train them to do the things we don't want them to do. I hope you are beginning to see that now.

Essentially, we unknowingly train our children to challenge us, ignore us, disrespect us and (in some cases) abuse us verbally and physically. *Parents have to realise children naturally have no boundaries.* Children are not adults with experience and judgement. They are self-centred, highly emotional beings who want everything now. It's our job as parents to socialise them so they know how to behave. If you're in the position of wearing the consequences of not understanding this when you first became a parent, I don't want you to be too hard on yourself. All is not lost. The fact you're reading this book means your intentions are good and you are up for the challenge of guiding and moulding your child's behaviour so they will understand how to behave without anyone having to get frustrated or yell at them all the time. The beauty of achieving this is they won't only know how to behave in the family unit – they will know how to behave out in public as well.

Managing the push back

Most children today aren't used to being expected to help at home, get off their devices, listen to your advice, go to bed on time or eat all their dinner. If this sounds like your children, you should probably expect some pushback as you work to give them more structure in their life. Resist the temptation to give in. If you don't insist on a better attitude from your children, then you can't be surprised if the pushback turns to resentment and morphs into manipulation.

You could consider the retraining process to be like a dance where you continue to lead no matter how wrong-footed your partner appears to be. Your children will eventually get to see it's no more difficult to learn how to grow up happily with respect than it is to push back all the time. In fact, they'll come to realise it's actually much easier.

Your goal is for everyone in the family to be accountable for keeping the home a happy place. Explaining this to your children will eventually result in positive behaviour becoming second nature to them. I don't say it won't be difficult, especially if you've been reigning over chaos for years. However, I do promise it is possible.

With 40 years of experience behind me, I can say without a shadow of a doubt that all children respond well to positive attention and strong, calm leadership. We only need to observe how children adore their coaches, trainers, dance teachers or anyone with authority who is teaching them how to be good at something. By being a present and strong parent, noticing what's really going on for your children, you will be in a position to raise conscious and curious children, who go on to become wonderful resourceful adults.

Managing aggressive behaviour

In the case of aggressive behaviour, you need to let your child know it's not acceptable and that they must stop it now. Your child must know you love them and nothing changes that. However, you are disciplining them so you and others can also 'like' them and enjoy their company without the fear of aggressive behaviour and continual, ineffective disciplining getting in the way.

To stop physically aggressive children, you will need to convince them you are stronger and more determined than they are. Do not be sweet or kind. Don't say anything like: Billy darling, it hurts Mummy when you hit her. This is not the time for terms of endearment. Hold the offending leg or arm firmly. If it's a small child, hold their body still – with your body if you must. Then wait. When the child realises you are in control, they will give up and cry. Once they do, you can say in a very firm and calm tone which is slightly louder than you would usually use: Never hit me or anyone again. Do you understand? Make sure you get acknowledgement. Until you do, keep asking: Do you understand? If necessary, add the word 'never' loudly, always looking them in the eye. This is not the time to start feeling sorry for them or making excuses for them. This is the time to teach them a lesson. Remember – you are doing this for them, not to them.

Managing the love bug

We all love our children. I've never met a parent who doesn't. We manage to love them no matter what they do. In *The Art of Growing Up* (2019), John Marsden says the problem today is 'we are seeing an epidemic of damaging parenting'. Marsden writes of the problematic state of 'parents being in love with their children, rather than loving them'.

The elephant in the room that most people don't talk about is that having children can rob us of our savings, isolate us from our friends who don't have children and make sleep-ins, Sunday brunches, movie nights and dinners out just too hard to get around to. The reality is that we had to give up some fabulous stuff to bring our first bundle of joy into the world. Nevertheless, we still love our children more than anything. But there is a catch here.
As Marsden says, 'We are limiting their ability to mature, and develop resilience and independence'.

If we're not completely aware, we can fall into the trap of giving in to thinking that providing our children with whatever they want and making excuses for their bad behaviour is what love looks like. Some parents just don't recognise this for what it really is – a kind of fear that our children won't love us if we are firm and don't allow them to have whatever they want.

We can also mistakenly think that love looks like over-protecting, over-parenting or over-organising our kids. If that sounds a little bit like you, I want to encourage you to try motivating, inspiring, prompting, exploring ideas, challenging, teaching and guiding – rather than doing and giving – as the new normal in your house.

When you look at the big picture and think about it, if you are over-organising, over-protecting and over-parenting, what are your children missing out on in the way of learning life skills? Perhaps take a minute right now and write down if your parenting could possibly be based on fear of any kind. If so, what are your kids missing out on when you're operating from fear?

I was guilty of doing too much for my children when they were young because of my desire to be needed. Living inside a loveless marriage had me craving more love from my children. This fear was driving my decisions and wasn't allowing my children the space and responsibility they needed to begin maturing into balanced, confident, responsible people. I am forever grateful to that mum who just planted the seed that prompted me to make new choices and snap out of fear, exhaustion and stress into my inner strength and leadership. Leadership meant being a great organiser rather than a servant to my children.

There's nothing wrong with getting children to help you pick up toys before the age of two. They can also make their beds by the time they're five and wash up from about the age of seven. Marsden despairs of parents who won't allow a four-year-old to peel a mandarin. Children are born ready to learn and it's our job as parents to teach, guide and inform them as they build the foundations from which to become wonderful adults.

The paradox is that we are doing our kids a terrible disservice when we love them too much and hinder their development. We can even stop them from trying to 'do better' when we praise every little 'nothing' they show us. Instead we should say: Hmmm, nice. Can you do a little neater next time, darling? I know you can! We don't want to say this every time of course, but certainly say it when you know they have not made any particular effort to do well. The problem with constant praise, and only praise, is the child has no reason to try harder. We all know that true self-esteem comes from trying hard, stretching ourselves, pushing through barriers and challenging ourselves to be the very best person we can be. Why wait to grow up before learning that?

There is a time for freedom and a time for restraint. Teaching both creates a more balanced adult. Naturally, the unconditional love we have for our children translates into our desire to make them happy. But there's another reason we must push our children to think about what they do. It's important not to praise kids for the sake of praising them because they probably know they don't deserve it. In fact, they probably find it disingenuous of you to be praising them or, even worse, having low standards for them. This may lead to your child wondering if you are being authentic with them about other things. At the end of the day, your good intentions to help your children build their self-esteem could have created the wrong impression altogether.

Giving in to our children is another situation that usually begins with good intentions but just ends up with children developing bad habits. Caught up in the moment and unable to see into the future, children want things now and they want them as if their life depends on getting them. We understand this because we sometimes feel that way, too. However, as a parent, if we don't put the work into remaining consciously aware, most of our responses to our children will be made in the moment for the moment. This robs them of learning opportunities and discipline. What I want you to do is start feeling more empowered. Let me fill you in on something author and 'confidence' coach, Anthony Robbins, teaches:

The one with the strongest conviction will win every time.

Make your convictions your 'musts' or at least make them stronger than your child's convictions when they are putting pressure upon you.

Managing the proceedings

Let's take a look at two seemingly innocent scenarios – where the kids end up in charge.

Scenario 1

You've arranged to pick your child up from their friend's house at 6 pm but when you arrive, they don't want to leave. You end up hanging around, making small talk with the other parents. The results are that the host family's dinner is being held up and you've missed the evening news, which you like to watch while the kids are having a bath. The delay in leaving has resulted in the evening routines of two families being pushed back.

Scenario 2

You've cooked a simple meal consisting of carrots, broccoli and chicken. Your child eats the chicken then complains he's full. The conversation goes as follows:

"Darling, just eat some of your veggies."

"I can't."

"Why?"

"I don't like them."

"Just a little, please."

"I'm full."

"Okay darling, but I want you to eat all your veggies tomorrow."

Ten minutes later, this happens:

"Can I have some ice cream, please Mummy?"

Thinking what lovely manners your child has, you say: "Yes. But tomorrow, promise me you'll eat all your veggies."

"Okay, Mummy."

Tomorrow never comes.

When giving in to our children, we may roll our eyes or mumble under our breath about just wanting a bit of peace but all that does is take a little bit of the sting out of the feeling in the pit of our stomach, knowing we could have done better. I don't want you to beat yourself up if what you've just read reminds you of you. I just want you to know you're creating a rod for your own back by giving in.

As easy as it is to give in to whatever your child so desperately wants, you need to know that what you're engaged in is a battle of wills. You are going to lose if you give in. What's more, letting your child win the battle is setting them up to lose the war. I'm saying this for two reasons:

- The rest of the world will not give in to your child the way you do.
- Your child is missing out on learning important lessons, beginning with learning resilience through disappointment.

As you can see, your best intentions may very well be backfiring because if you don't turn things around quickly, you are likely to find you have created a fragile, easily hurt, self-centred child who cannot take feedback of any kind from anyone. Worse still, you may have even created a narcissistic child or someone who lacks the wherewithal to develop into a fully mature adult. No-one wins.

Managing readiness

If your child wants to do things they have no hope of achieving, or aren't mature enough to even attempt, you should simply say: No darling, you are not ready for that yet. Soon you will be ready though. This response allows them to feel the joy of anticipation and avoid the moodiness and frustration that can result from the feeling of disappointment they experience when they try something and fail.

I've seen this scenario hundreds of times – children trying to tie their shoelaces, put on their seatbelt, or plait their hair before they have the manual dexterity they need. They don't know that, though, and they wind up frustrated and whining and out of control when their attempts at doing these things fail. You can avoid this by letting them know you will be doing these things for them for now and when they're ready, you'll teach them how to do it for themselves. End of story. Delivering this information with a firm tone will not break their little hearts. It will show them, once again, that all is well because you know what you're doing.

It can be a major problem for children if parents want to please them more than they want to teach them. It's time for parents to see that teaching things like patience and respect is a much better gift for children than caving in to their demands so they don't get upset. When children don't have an appreciation of the importance of considering you and your needs, they will struggle to consider the needs of others when they grow up. The good news is if you encourage children to be thoughtful and listen to what you are telling them, they will develop the capacity to be patient and considerate and will also be less stressed and disappointed when things don't go their way.

Managing decision-making

Until children have enough information and life experience to make logical decisions, you should be making decisions for them. There's a very good reason why they can't sign the papers for a mortgage, get a driver's licence, or make sensible choices like eating broccoli rather than sugar-filled cereal all the time.

Children are driven by their urges and passions. They live in the present moment. Reasoning with them will only get you so far and asking them what they want can often lead to you having to change their mind. The simple fact is that children are not equipped to make better decisions than you are. When children focus their energy on having fun, helping at home and doing their best at school, without even noticing it they are building their capacity to be a great decision-maker when they grow up. This doesn't mean they can't make a decision every now and then or offer a different option to the one you are proposing. If they are generally being well-behaved, there's no harm in you being open to discussion sometimes. What children should definitely not be doing, though, is getting into the habit of being argumentative and battling with you all day long over every decision you make.

It's a bit of a balancing act. Healthy growth entails children constantly testing their environment. They want to know how the world works, what their boundaries are and what they can and can't get away with. That's only natural. As responsible adults in a world where 'control' and 'discipline' have become dirty words, we need to have enough presence of mind and confidence to know when boundaries need to be firmly maintained, as opposed to a time when the child has developed enough emotional maturity for the boundaries to be moved.

No matter what today's psychology around giving choices to children is, trust me when I say your children learn important lessons by watching and listening to you. What that means is that you have to be on the ball and consistent. You also need to model integrity. There is no point in telling your six-year-old son he is amazing and wonderful one minute, when the next minute you're opening up to a friend on the phone saying he's driving you crazy. Children love eavesdropping, so you need to be very careful. It won't matter if you tell your six-year-old how clever he is 100 times a day because he won't forget you told your friend he was a little monster. What's even worse is he may never feel he can fully trust you again. He doesn't have the maturity to figure out that maybe you just had a hard day and were just letting off steam. He won't know you still love and adore him even when he does act like a little monster.

Reward charts

A simple way to reinforce progress in things that matter, like thoughtfulness, is to acknowledge them. Rewards charts are a wonderful way to do that. Be as creative as you like with the way you set these up. To the best of your ability, make the goals you are setting for your children both specific and attainable. That way, it's easy for both of you to know when they've been reached and it's time to get a reward.

If there is only one child involved, it's all about getting them to compete against themselves. In the case of two or more children, you need to make sure the older child doesn't have an unfair advantage over the younger ones. To avoid the younger one feeling hopeless because they are constantly being beaten, make sure you make the goals relevant to each child's level of development.

How and when to reward your children

These days, material possessions and treats of other kinds are usually given freely to kids, who often don't appreciate them. Having to save up or earn the right to have treats seems an old-fashioned way to do things. The kinds of environments I see when I'm brought in to help families thrive, are ones where children are used to taking whatever they can get their hands on. They then go on to demand the next thing. This is such a shame as children get great joy from receiving something they have earned.

If you're thinking that the idea of getting your kids to 'earn' their treats isn't going to work in your house, I want you to give it a try first. I'm really backing myself here because I know charging things up and drip-feeding treats allows children to experience the buzz of anticipation that comes with looking forward to receiving something they have had to earn. This gives them a true sense of pride.

Not everyone may agree but I find rewarding children with money, if they don't have to be reminded to do their jobs or if they make outstanding gestures to help others, is a great motivator that will instil the habit of good behaviour in the child. What I like most about the concept is, although it's usually just a matter of a few dollars each week, the money earned can be saved up for something the child really wants without having to wait for a birthday. You might even consider doing a deal where the children only have to earn half the cost of something more expensive and you put in the balance.

Of course the child's age needs to be taken into consideration. For children in the 6 to 10-year-old age group, rewards can be effective.

You can offer cash for things like:

- consistently being kind and patient
- feeding the dog
- washing up
- putting away the dishes
- weeding the garden
- making their bed each day
- doing their homework without being asked
- vacuuming a room
- washing the car
- keeping their bedroom tidy.

Other rewards that work include:

- one-on-one dinner dates with a parent
- movie nights at home or the theatre
- half an hour extra access to PlayStation, tablet or phone.

If you are using a chart, you can add a tick for every good deed and remove one for every bad deed. At the end of the week, add up the ticks to see the results and the rewards and celebrate with your child.

Managing hovering and fixing

There are obviously times when you need to be on top of a situation and step in, such as when you have a very small child who is at the mercy of a biter, if a primary school child is lacking the skills to defend themselves against a bully and especially if your teenager has hooked up with an unsavoury character. However, a lot of the time you can take a step back and allow your children to safely develop coping skills of their own.

The trick is to be aware and observe. By all means, step in if your child is not coping. Even if you have to step in, you are still helping them develop important coping skills while being on their side. Important skills for children to have are the ability to bounce back if they feel upset by something, saying 'back off' if someone is bullying them and taking the initiative to choose friends rather than always waiting to be chosen. How your children deal with these situations comes down to knowing what to do and practising doing it. Soon they will gain confidence and not let things upset them as much because they know they are okay and capable alone.

Essentially parenting is about teaching, more than it is about doing. Helping your child to learn about being respectful, responsible, polite and thoughtful will give them some of the skills they need to get on in the world. Teaching our children about life in a way that empowers them, rather than making them dependent on us, is what parenting is all about.

Managing instant gratification addiction

Addiction to the instant gratification delivered by handheld devices is robbing families of real connection and robbing children of the ability to appreciate the little but important things in life. It's also making it all but impossible for children to choose to go for a walk instead of opening up one of the social media channels they are subscribed to. What's more, it's robbing everyone of opportunities to socialise together and get the benefits of interacting with human beings who are spending actual real time together.

I want to share a story that highlights what I'm saying. Recently, I was walking the dog at about 8.30 in the morning, watching some young kids on bikes in a group. I started talking to them and found out they were waiting for a couple of their friends before heading off. Not a device in sight. I also noticed a mum with three young children riding their bikes behind her. I overheard the 7-year-old boy saying something slightly judgemental to the younger girl.

The mum quickly said: Don't speak to your sister that way. The boy then humbly said: Sorry Mum. This really took me by surprise as so many kids I've met recently would just have ignored her.

What I've noticed when I take one of my regular trips out of the city to see my daughter who lives in a quiet spot near the beach, is that this environment seems to create happier families, where children are much more comfortable chatting and spending less time on technology. It breaks my heart to see fractured relationships in families, because children spend too much time in front of screens and become agitated or even nasty when their devices are taken away from them. That's why I recommend keeping devices as a treat to be earned rather than only using the confiscation of devices as a punishment.

Having devices in prams, in beds and on dining tables may well be a strategy that works to keep the kids quiet – but at what cost? It's huge! We are actually eroding the quality of life with millions of tiny bits of information delivered in bright colours and funky noises, bombarding our children's brains. The fact that children get upset when their devices are taken away is a sure sign they are addicted.

By the way, addictions are also formed when parents and caregivers hand things like food, toys, entertainment or compliments over to children just to get some peace. Again, if your child is already thinking about what's next with an underlying sense of agitation and dissatisfaction, then unfortunately you've primed them to be dissatisfied with life because you're giving them too much.

Imagine how much more gratifying life would be if you replaced 'things' with some good old-fashioned undivided attention. You'd really know how your child is doing and they'd get to know how great it feels to have real conversations with someone who is looking them in the eye.

Even if your child is attached to a screen every spare moment right now, what they really want is more of you. They just don't know it yet. If the screen has replaced you, it's time to get tough and take the screen away. Make the tough decisions now and your child will thank you one day when they are out in the world and noticing they have the kind of interpersonal skills and confidence so many people can only dream of – all because you had the courage to do what needed to be done.

If your children become moody, angry or stressed at the prospect of you taking their phone away from them for a day, then that's exactly what you should do. They might hate you in the moment but they will not stop loving you.

The bottom line is that tough love creates strong resilient children while passive parenting creates weak unhappy ones. I hear so many parents excuse turning a blind eye to their children's faults, by saying things like, 'It's the times we live in' or 'All kids are doing it' or 'They need it for their homework'. These are permissive statements people are using to alleviate guilt. If you're doing this, you need to stop and consider whether you might actually be a little bit addicted yourself. If you are, I feel for you. This stuff is real and I recommend you become willing to stop or get some help. In the absence of that, you might look into getting a creative hobby of some kind and become a student of mindfulness. You'll find a chapter on this very subject in Part 3.

I care a lot about this topic because our addiction to technology and social media doesn't just mean we are relying on the dopamine hit we get when we see a 'like' on one of our posts. It also means we need it just to feel OK. The big picture is horrifying. Don't let your kids or yourself be statistics.

Managing manipulation

Genuine sadness needs comfort, whereas put-on sadness a child might be using get their own way is a completely different situation. If you don't want your kids to conjure up fake emotions to express their desires, you'll need to teach them how to communicate their needs without losing the plot or pretending to lose it. What you don't want to do is encourage your child to get into the habit of relating sadness to attention and affection. This is where we really need to be conscious, tuned-in and sensitive to the particular situation at hand.

To begin responding in a more helpful and healthier way, you can stop encouraging sadness by teaching coping skills to your kids. First, make a connection with your child – a touch, say their name and give a smile when they look at you. Begin by saying something like the following:

> *Because I love you, I can see the difference between you actually being sad/angry/frustrated and when you're just trying to get your own way. Crying and yelling is not how you need to deal with things, darling. Let me help you to find another way.*
>
> *Sometimes you can just come and talk to me and tell me what's going on with you and sometimes you have to just listen to me. I have to teach you how to handle whatever you're feeling. So when Mummy says no and you don't*

like it, it's no good screaming at me or crying. That just makes you upset and me angry. So let's find another way.

Another thing you can say is:

I'm here for you but I won't let you cry and be angry at me because you want your own way.

If you're having these kinds of talks, teaching communication skills and the confidence to know when and how to use them, you will be setting your child up for an easier and more conscious life.

I don't know too much about neuroplasticity but I do know that if children get to a state where they get a dopamine rush from the attention they get when they are upset, they are potentially being set up to be one of those people we've probably all met – the person who thrives on drama. The whole thing behind addiction is the dopamine hit. You don't want your child growing up thinking of sadness as comforting. Now is the time for them to be learning how to manage their emotions in a way that isn't going to compromise their wellbeing.

The fact is that kids don't want to be told what to do but they do want to learn.

It's only natural that they push back a little but don't give in and let them off the hook. Instead, get smart and teach them how to do things. Help them feel good about doing things they'd prefer not to be doing – like their homework or loading the dishwasher – without having to be asked. The trick to behaviour modification is to never back down. As long as you remain more committed to your outcome than the child is to theirs, their behaviour will eventually get better. Things might get loud but don't give in and it will soon be easy.

Manage your fear of being judged

As a parent, it's your responsibility to do whatever needs to be done, when it needs to be done and how it needs to be done. Most parents I've worked with have fallen into the habit of indulging their children to stop them from crying or carrying on when they're out and about with others. I know how easy it is to fall into that trap but it's important that you are not dissuaded from taking the action you need to take to be consistent with your child about what is and isn't appropriate behaviour – even if a bystander is looking at you and obviously judging you when you look like your ignoring your child who is throwing a tantrum at the supermarket.

Your fear of judgement is what your children will see when they act out at the supermarket and you decide to placate them because you are afraid of what other people will think if you let them carry on until they run out of energy. It's pointless then telling them to go to their room to sit in silence and think about their behaviour when they get home.

What you're working against in the beginning is the fact you've always given into your children in the past. So the first time you decide things have to change, you're likely to be in for a very uncomfortable hour or so of them carrying on. Sooner rather than later, your child will see you mean business and that they might as well just fall into line.

If you're holding your power and letting your child throw a tantrum without responding or giving them any energy or attention, people will stare – that's a given. But believe me when I say some of them will actually be admiring you because, essentially, what you're doing is showing your child you won't be bullied. I would be surprised if it ever happens again but if it does, you know what to do. Soon it will stop.

When it comes to leadership and life in general, success is achieved by doing the things we don't really want to do, rather than avoiding them. You're going to have to suck up any discomfort you're experiencing in the supermarket, or wherever you happen to be, and hold your ground. The quality of your child's life depends on it. This might not be easy but it is too important to worry about whether some of the other people at the supermarket conclude that the tantrum means you are not in control. In fact they'd be totally wrong because, in this case, the tantrum means you are in control.

Managing disrespect

Help your child feel how important it is for your family to run harmoniously with everyone understanding the governing rules. The most essential governing rule is mutual respect – it adds credence to your reprimands in relation to any disrespectful behaviour you pick up on. There may still be times when you have to raise your voice but nipping things in the bud immediately is a great way to prevent annoying behaviours from becoming habits, or to stop them if they already have.

Children are actually quite brilliant, you know. They can spot a phoney a mile off. So you can't afford to be saying one thing and doing something else. You need to find your inner strength and jump on bad behaviour, bad responses, and bad moods or actions as soon as you see the first flicker of disrespect. What's more, you want to always demonstrate self-respect as a model for your children to follow. Having self-respect means you won't stand for disrespectful words or behaviour from anyone. As a conscious parent, by always expecting respect from others, you show you would never accept anything less from your children.

Weekly family meetings

Weekly family meeting can speed up the changes you need to make. With every member of the family present, you will help keep everyone connected and on the same page. These meetings are not only about managing the logistics of the busy lives that all of us lead, but they are also an opportunity for everyone to share their life journey within the family and outside of it, on an ongoing basis.

The goal of each meeting is for everyone to sit together, to take time to communicate their feelings, to contribute to the creation of rules, discuss family values that they want to live by, and celebrate their love and appreciation for their family. Above all, it's about having some fun along the way. This is a space where children and parents can find comfort, knowing that they'll be listened to and understood by the people who love them the most in the world.

It's important that everybody attends, no matter what age they are. And it's also important that they don't have any devices with them. When I say 'attend' here, I really mean 'attend'. Among other things, these meetings are great opportunities for people who are learning about maintaining healthy boundaries.

And of course, being polite and listening to others and not talking over the top of them is an important boundary to maintain during these meetings.

On the most practical level, family meetings help with the organisation of the day-to-day running of the household. Hopefully, they will put an end to a situation that I see a lot of families falling into where chores and schedules get piled on top of everything else that mum and dad have to do. These meetings are to help everyone acknowledge and contribute to everything that it takes to run a family.

It's best if everyone has a pen and paper to write down notes from the meeting, capturing everything they need to be aware of, and take responsibility for. This could be dental appointments, dress-up day at school, chores, homework, morning routines and anything and everything family members need to be aware of. Family meetings can be run with an agenda that addresses everything happening that week so there's more order and everyone knows how to take responsibility for their own 'stuff' while accepting there needs to be fairness in the way responsibilities are shared around.

I think you might be surprised when you hear some of the solutions and see how enthusiastic children become when they have a say in how they can contribute to the smooth running of the family.

The trick in all of this is finding tasks that are age appropriate and are all seen as equally valuable. This is important because even a 2-year-old needs to be enthusiastically acknowledged for their contribution.

It's important you are patient and teach the little ones (and the older ones, if they need it), how to do what you're expecting them to do. Show them with little step-by-step instructions. This is a fabulous way for your child to gain confidence, independence and pride in a job well done.

I've also found reading together prior to a meeting – especially if you can dream up a family story or have had stories handed down from your grandparents – can open up a child's heart and help them to want to contribute more willingly. I encourage reading stories that contain a moral or a virtue you'd like to instil in your children. This can be quite a lovely and enjoyable exercise the family can do together. It is a positive way to open up dialogue where everyone feels as if their contribution matters and being a part of your family also matters.

The first family meeting will need to address what's been working to keep the family running smoothly to date, as well as what hasn't been working so well and what can be done to improve things. This is also an opportunity for the family rules to be discussed and, most importantly, agreed on.

Once you've run your first meeting and established things like the rules and an understanding of boundaries, you could follow an agenda each week that looks a bit like this one:

1. Welcome
2. Recognition of good behaviour and any rewards due
3. Recognition of what didn't go so well and how we can improve (including conversations)
4. Assignment of any household chores that need to be allocated
5. Organisation of all school and extracurricular activities, including putting the dates into a calendar that sits on the fridge or somewhere else easily viewed

Before we move on from family meetings, I want to share a lovely story which took place when I was helping a family I was working with get better organised. At the very first meeting, it emerged that the 4-year-old child, who was notorious for daydreaming, was finding it hard to get ready for school every morning. I can still see how proud this little angel was when he came up with an idea that was so good his sister decided she would take it up as well. He proposed he should put on his school uniform after his evening bath and sleep in it so he only had to do four things when he woke up in the morning – pull up his bedclothes, put his lunch in his bag, eat his breakfast and clean his teeth.

That was one of the best outcomes of a family meeting I've seen because there was a moment there where I saw that 4-year-old child understand he has the power to solve problems all on his own. We can't overestimate how helpful that is in a child's development.

Managing sleep

To get enough sleep yourself, you must have children listening to you at bedtime – no excuses. I have to admit, because I worked such long hours, I played with my children until 7.30 pm then we all went off to bed. The four of us fell asleep in my bed and when I woke around 9 pm, I would take them, one by one, to their own rooms. There were periods when this didn't happen and because the children were used to doing what they were told and were flexible, they were happy to go to bed on their own and go straight to sleep when they were told to.

The first principle is that 20 minutes of quiet non-stimulating activity works brilliantly at priming children's bodies to fall asleep.

At 7 pm, start a routine of brushing teeth, calmly listening to the day's highlights, then a story and song. Children will soon realise this routine is followed by lights out until the time they're used to waking up. What's important here is consistency and commitment. Just say: Good night, darling. I'll see you when the sun comes up. Love you so much. Kiss kiss. Then leave. Do not answer any questions. Everything after that is just a manipulation so do not respond.

If that doesn't work for whatever reason, you'll have to add some extra strategies such as:

- Keep your child's bed exclusively for sleep. This entails having cuddles and reading somewhere other than on the bed.
- Set an alarm for 7 pm and treat that as a non-negotiable time, saying: Bedtime now.
- Get a cuddly toy that is only for bedtime and treat it as the transition object with a personality just like yours so your children feel happy when you leave them because they have a 'replacement' to snuggle up with.

Other strategies include dressing your child in loose clothing, keeping the room cool and keeping the bed free of any items, except for the cuddly toy. If fear of the dark is an issue for your children, have a conversation with them about how safe they are. Stand at the doorway with your child on a chair. Get your child to turn the light on, have a look around the room, turn the light off and look around again.

That's when you can say: See darling, it's exactly the same. The light is having a sleep too. That's all!

If necessary, use a dull light by the bed so the room is not completely black. You could go shopping together for the light, priming them to feel comfortable in bed by talking about how their fears will go away as soon as the dull light comes on.

Remember, your children will only know how to deal with their feelings if you teach them. If your child has a fear around you not returning once you leave the room, during daylight hours you could play a game where you all have to count while you go away for a few seconds then come back. That way, you show them you'll still be in the house, even if they can't see you.

If you have inadvertently trained your child to expect that all they need to do is call out and you'll come into the room, then you need to untrain them by ignoring their calls, even though it might feel terrible at first. Explain to the children you have things to do and it is bedtime for the kids. Then say: You're okay, just close your eyes, rock a little and before you know it, you're asleep.

Managing meal times

Mealtimes are a time for nourishment and connection. Helping your child enjoy food is easy if you start giving them a variety of normal foods from 12 months of age and consider the following points:

- Hungry children will eat anything, so make sure you don't allow them the luxury of convincing you what they will and won't eat.
- Never offer an alternative to what you are serving for dinner.
- If your child says they don't like something, just remind them it's really good for their body and that they need to eat it anyway – in a no-nonsense voice.
- If your child doesn't want to eat dinner then it's probably time to stop giving them afternoon snacks and start serving dinner earlier.
- Don't end every meal with something sweet.
- As a last resort, if your child is used to being fussy at dinner time and you just can't find a way around it, give them all the nutrition they need in snack form, during the day, until the child is old enough to reason with.
- Make the child feel disadvantaged if they decide they are not sitting at the dinner table with the family.
- Don't offer food after dinner time is finished unless they ate all their dinner.
- Don't beg and plead for them to eat – this is a power game you will lose. Just move them away from the table and say: Off you go.

When they ask for food later, say: Sorry, you missed out. They won't die of starvation and tomorrow, they will eat dinner.

Managing tantrums

Children resort to out-of-control behaviours, such as tantrums, because they haven't been shown a better way to deal with their feelings. Teaching them a better way to deal with their feelings can start at around 12 months of age.

The first time a tantrum begins, ignore it. As long as your child is safe, walk away. Do this three times and it should stop for good. If not, become aware of your child's lead-up to a tantrum and try to nip that in the bud. Watch for the signs which may include:

- changes in breathing
- a funny look
- face turning red
- whining and wriggling
- all of the above.

Be calm and firm and say: Stop it, NOW! Get down to their level, put your arm around them, make them aware of what they're doing and tell them you can fix it together. If you can't calm them down that way, then you need to physically help their body to get still so they aren't winding themselves up physically as well as emotionally. I find singing loudly while performing the octopus act settles the child more quickly.

Children want and need to know someone is smarter than them, stronger than them and loves them enough to get them through these awful times. If children feel overpowered by their emotions and no-one is helping them understand they are controllable, then it is only natural their emotions will take over. The earlier children start learning self-control, the better.

Managing hitting and biting

It's as simple as this. If you stop an 8 to 12-month-old from hitting you and biting, you won't have a 2 to 6-year-old attacking you, or a 14-year-old for that matter. No child should ever be permitted to hit or bite their parents, or anyone else. It is not okay – ever. Remember, you are programming your child for life so follow the points below to set things straight.

- Say STOP loudly and emphatically – it won't hurt if they get a little shocked.
- Look into their eyes.
- Pull them off you.
- Show them you mean it by looking disgusted.
- Do whatever it takes, within reason, to get the message through that this is not acceptable.
- Avoid words of endearment and a compassionate tone.

Never allow this abuse towards you to happen without consequences. It's not as if the children have spilled milk or accidentally made a mistake. They are attacking you and it has to be stopped.

Managing teenagers and pre-teens

As children get older, there are many things you can take away from them if respect is not forthcoming. Teenagers, especially, feel they know it all and can do whatever they wish, despite their parents' rules. This will be more likely if they've been handed over the power for most of their lives. But believe it or not, teenagers can be well-behaved, polite and happy. In fact, when they are around 16 and 17, we need to appreciate this is a time when they are preparing themselves to be able to think and live independently. Of course, 16 and 17-year-olds were once 9 and 10-year-olds.

I despair when I see 10-year-olds being moody and morose. In many cases, they've picked these habits up from TV shows or other kids. Many parents think this is a part of growing up and only to be expected, but I don't agree. I believe allowing moodiness is damaging children's mental health as well as the quality of their relationships.

Managing moods and enabling respect

As parents, we need to help our children think in ways that serve them – not in ways that predispose them to negativity and possibly depression. It's our job to show them how to find solutions to any problems they're experiencing and how to look for joy in life.

The way we go about choosing our thoughts is a habit, and just like any of the other ones, we know we can change if they are not good for us. Swearing is a particularly unhelpful and somewhat burgeoning trend at the moment. Let's be honest, it's all around us so if little children are swearing, they more than likely picked it up from us. If you've been swearing in front of your children, simply tell them you're going to stop it now because it is a tricky habit that has snuck up on you and it's actually very rude.

Most teenagers can and will be positive at school but moody at home. I've heard parents say they are holding it all together for others and need to let their feelings out at home. However, the truth is they can learn to think of more supportive and self-sustaining ways than that. Retraining a teenager isn't any harder than retaining a toddler – you just have to provide enough reasons for them to want to be their best.

As little screen time as possible will help a lot. I especially dislike the violent games kids are likely to be playing until all hours, leaving them to get up in the morning seriously sleep deprived. They could even end up compulsively lying to you because they've become addicted to the adrenaline hit they get from these games. This is not a positive way to live. Weekly family meetings, loving conversations and doing fun things together as a family will help kids get out of their head and into the moment. This is incredibly important for them, mentally and emotionally.

It's important you don't let your rebelling child have the last word, especially while they're in retraining mode. Teenagers have often been heard to say: I don't care if you're mad at me. But the truth is – they do. So don't think ignoring disrespectful behaviour will be the best option.

There are times when it's really important not to parent from our heartstrings. We need to lead with strength and a commitment to do whatever it takes to help our children not be a pain to be around. You are making decisions for the long term here – for everybody's good, especially your child's. Many parents of teenagers give in to their children because it's easier in the moment and they don't want whatever is going on to ramp up. However, if you continually give in, you're only exacerbating the problem, empowering the child and being of no benefit to their development as a good person.

Make sure to follow through with discipline at all times. Never give in if you get pressured. If you're persistent, in no time at all they'll begin to give in and stop arguing over every little thing because it's more enjoyable to keep within the rules. Remember you are coming from a place of teaching them how the world works. They are coming from a place of instant gratification and me-oriented choices. You must win every battle. There's a lot at stake here. By giving in you encourage more challenging behaviours that could end up seeing you pick them up from a police station one day.

Teenagers and pre-teens are usually really savvy and have ways of finding a loophole that even makes you question yourself sometimes. I implore you not to get sucked in to that merry-go-round they call 'their opinion'. Just don't go there. If you get to the point where you need to walk away from their challenges, you could sign off with a definitive statement such as 'no-one cares' or 'because I said so'.

Once you put the work into establishing rules and boundaries, loving communication and connection will be your family's default mode. If your child is pushing back, then you must take the lead and be firm, letting them know conversations around what they want will only be heard when they are showing respect and not when they are challenging you.

Many parents forget to focus on the big picture. The long-term effects of disrespect are damaging in so many ways – not least of all being your child's trust. If you are thinking that giving in will help your relationship with your child, then think again. Your child will need your advice and help throughout their life but they won't turn to you if they know you can be manipulated by a child.

The strength and courage you show now will be how they learn these qualities and enjoy them as adults. Your child is not learning anything by overpowering you, except how to be a bully. More important than anything else is to create a relationship built on trust and respect.

PART 2

Seeing the family as a TEAM

CHAPTER 5: TRUST

Trust is the fruit of the relationship in which you know you are loved.
— William Paul Young

I have a simple, yet profound message for you here. Trust is established by the hundred and one little things we do on a daily basis.

So, you should be honest with what you say. End of story. Don't say you like something if you really don't. And if you don't care about something, don't pretend you do.

Similarly, don't tell kids to do something and not follow up if they don't do it. At the same time, if something isn't important to you then don't bother making it a rule. Before jumping in with guns blazing, it's always a good idea to ask yourself – Is this important to me? If it's not really important, then let it go. There's no need for you to conform to anyone else's idea of what matters.

Sticking to your rules is much easier when there aren't a million of them. Be firm on the things that matter and relaxed on the things that don't.

Say what you mean and mean what you say

Your child is watching you every minute of every day. They are listening to everything you say. If you make a habit of saying things you don't follow through on, your child will soon work out your word means very little and they will get into the habit of trying to persuade you to give in to them all the time. For example, you may have said they have to eat all the food on their plate if they want dessert, but they've left the cabbage. Maybe you didn't like cabbage yourself as a child and you decide to give in – just this once – because you can understand where they're coming from.

Make no mistake about it – this kind of inconsistency will undo you.

I'll say it again – it's really important you stick to your guns. This might sound inconsequential in the wider scheme of things but not holding the line ultimately gives children the idea there are shifting goalposts and it takes away any sense of security around knowing what is expected of them and their ability to trust you to do what you say you will.

As unimportant as giving in over something inconsequential can seem in the moment, it's important to remember your life is made up of these moments.

Let's face it, some kids are easier than others to teach but that doesn't mean you need to give in more – quite the opposite. A wilful child will try to convince you to say yes every time they want something. The moral of this story is that when you say that something is a rule, or you tell your children to do something, you need to do your utmost to enforce it. There will be times when you just can't. Make it clear that this is because you see the benefit in the changes – not that you are giving in or backing down. This way, you still get to keep your position as the leader and decision-maker.

The importance of togetherness

Members of a happy family love spending time together. When your children are engaged enjoy being involved in what you're doing, life is just easier and much more fun. Family activities and chores done with the right attitude can be really enjoyable, so put on some music and sing as you do the chores together. Your child will sometimes say: I don't want to. If this happens, just use your best cheerful, 'no-nonsense' voice and reply: Put on a happy face and let's get going. From a very young age, this helps children realise you are all in this together as a family. As they say in the classics – a family that plays together stays together.

This is your family. Your team. These are the people who, without a doubt, you can trust to do the right thing. This may need to be drummed into your children if they've got in the habit of not wanting to spend time with you or help you. The upside of chores is they give us a chance to have some bonding time together. This will go a long way to giving your children an interest in life and what goes on around them because they are learning to engage and help others, making them happier, more content and even less bored. They will also feel genuinely proud of who they are and a whole lot more capable than a child who has everything done for them. Finally, because they are more competent, they will also be less demanding.

Affection is what affection does

Affection and family go hand in hand in my book. If you came from an affectionate family, you would notice you felt really loved. Knowing how much your family loved you gave you a feeling that you were part of a special team working together, warts and all. It's worth noting that affection is not always physical. It can manifest in a feeling you have when you're together with the people you like a lot and love.

Children who have no regard for boundaries and misbehave all the time are likely to miss out on this feeling. That's not to say that we withhold affection from them on purpose. It's just that a child who is constantly disrespecting you and losing the plot all the time is unlikely to inspire spontaneous affection. In a sense, everyone misses out because it's just as lovely to give affection as it is to receive it.

It's also important to note that misbehaviour does not inhibit love at all. Love is a deep abiding state. Affection, on the other hand, is more of an 'in the moment' experience that inspires a hug, a wink, a pat on the back or even just a smile. When you look at your child with a smile or give them an affectionate touch or hug, endorphins are released. Apart from making you feel great, this creates the perfect environment for learning and bonding to happen.

In helping your kids with boundaries, you'll find almost all children really want to be good but they often carry on because they haven't been taught how to deal with their feelings in a way that helps them to process them and to handle themselves better. Basically, children just don't know how to behave if they haven't been taught. So, it's not their fault if they don't feel like being affectionate towards you.

Once you find your family's comfortable and unique balance of affection, fun and firmness, then you will have set the scene for an enjoyable family life where trust is the glue that holds it all together. It's almost impossible to have respect without trust, so if your child refuses to be respectful you will have to open up a conversation to find out if somewhere they lost trust in you.

Working as a team

Today's family operates very differently to the way families lived twenty or so years ago. So much has changed, especially expectations around what it means to be a mum or a dad. These days, many dads and mums are home with children as well as running a business, or they're juggling several roles in between doing everything that needs to be done each day for the family. Some head off to work every day. Many mothers and some dads are working full time and trying to fit in parenting without a partner, while performing all the other tasks needed to keep on top of things. The 'traditional' family of two parents with mum home and dad working is now more rare than common. Single parenting is also a growing demographic.

Unlike when my parents brought me up, most parents these days are doing what they do without help from the extended family. All the while, they're trying to hold it all together and not be (or seem to be) stressed or feeling guilty about not having more time to spend with the kids. However, more often than not, parents and children are suffering with stress and anxiety on a daily basis.

It's obvious there's more going on for families than ever before. Overwhelm is at an all-time high. Even though every parent is doing their best, most are struggling. When desperate families call me to help them sort things out, I don't hesitate to acknowledge they are actually doing pretty well given there's way too much for everyone to handle. It's great they've called me in to help because the pressures are not going to go away by themselves. The only way to deal with them is to get everyone on board and on the same page, working together as a TEAM.

I don't know if this is your experience but a lot of families argue over doing the household chores. In case you're wondering, it's not all your job to do! Children can feel resentment about having to help and most parents feel overwhelmed by the enormous workload. This is where great leadership really makes a difference. Every team needs a great leader. Leadership in the form of parenting is not very different from being a leader of anything. The qualities are the same – confidence, commitment to outcomes, great communication skills, tenacity and trustworthiness. A sense of humour and theatrics can go a long way as well.

If you manage to really connect with your children and get them to appreciate the importance of getting on board with you as their leader, they are much more likely to want to make a genuine contribution to the family team.

I really worry about the incredibly high levels of anxiety and stress I see in families these days. This has to change if our children are going to avoid the predictions of child psychologists and other experts about the state families are in, flagging an unhealthy escalation in the incidence of childhood mental disorders, disruptive behaviours, such as temper tantrums, and many other conditions that make life harder than need be.

Much of this can be avoided when children are feeling more connected and supported. It's not about pandering to their seemingly fragile egos – that doesn't help – it's about engaging them and helping them to genuinely feel good about themselves. Being committed to every member of the team and making decisions that benefit everyone is essential to foster connection.

According to Dr Tim Sharp, Chief Happiness Officer with The Happiness Institute, the happiest people are those who belong to a tribe and contribute to the tribe. Working together for a cause, even if it's just your family, with the right attitude can be fun and gratifying. Feeling loved and loving each other is the antidote to what isn't working in families these days. I promise you, when all of these things come together, harmony in your family is almost guaranteed. Surely that's worth making it a priority?

CHAPTER 6: ENJOYMENT

Life must be lived as a play.
— Plato

You may think, as a parenting expert I consider parenting to be deadly serious and all about the rules and logistics and all the other business needed to run a family. That's true enough, I guess, but the reverse is also true. While parenting is a serious matter, it's also one of the most fun things that anyone could possibly opt for. Let's face it, if we're lucky, it's for the rest of our lives, so making it enjoyable has to be a priority.

Making the decision to enjoy parenting just makes sense to me. After all, you're shaping lives when you bring children into the world and raise them to become fully-fledged adults. Childhood is seen as the formative years for a very good reason – it determines how we see the world and ourselves in that world. That's why it's important we make sure we do more teaching and guiding, and less spoiling of our children so we have more stress-free time to laugh and play.

CHAPTER 6: ENJOYMENT

Parenting is an incredible gift and responsibility. Get it wrong by giving the child all love and no boundaries, for example, and you may wind up with an unemployable tyrant on your hands by the time they're twenty. On the other hand, if you give children too many boundaries and not enough space to learn by trial and error, you're likely to wind up with a rebellious person on your hands who has no respect for you and certainly doesn't want any more of your input into their lives.

If you are firm and loving and you can hold your ground every time you have to put your foot down about something, you will soon need to put your foot down less and less. Quite simply your child soon realises that when you say something, it's not said to stand over them or bully them. It's actually because you know what's best for them as part of the family. This is how they begin to appreciate you are a great leader – because you can see the bigger picture that they cannot. Getting to that point makes parenting so much more fun.

Raising children with fun and firmness means they will respect you for the rest of your life. What's more, your child will grow into the sort of person that everyone (including you) wants to spend time with. They'll be capable, thriving on love, helpful and conscious. The great thing about all this is once you have the framework, with rules and boundaries in place, and once you've got yourself into a state where you can be a calm loving leader, rather than the chauffeur or the personal assistant, then you can really start to focus on the fun stuff and on enjoying every moment together.

The key to a happy life is to be fun, loving and inquisitive. As the leader of your family, you need to be at the top of your game. That doesn't mean you can't also be fun and relaxed. To do this, you'll need an open mind. You'll need to ease into an awareness that becoming a parent means you will have to continually adapt, evolve and grow. And you'll also need to embrace and enjoy your role. Finding the right balance between being a fun and loving parent and a focused and attentive one is the perfect tonic for ailing families.

Children respond incredibly positively when they feel as though their parents are relaxed, focused and have it all in hand. I'll let you in on a little secret here – even if you're not, you have my permission to fake it while you make it. For me, one of the most enjoyable parts of parenting and raising children is the ability to use theatrics to get your point across – kids just love it.

Have you ever noticed how we tend to mimic others? This is a natural unconscious response, called mirroring. Nowhere is this more evident than with children and their parents. I'm sure this isn't you, but if parents are moody and unmotivated TV-watching couch potatoes who find little joy in life, then more likely than not their children will wind up with much the same attitude. Whereas if parents are happy, inquisitive, energetic types who are interested in learning and loving life, then their children will likely feel the same way – they will find life exciting, interesting and full of colour, knowing it's to be enjoyed.

If you find your child has an attitude you don't like, I suggest you start by looking at yourself to see if you ever project that sort of attitude without realising it. If you do, it's time to take a long hard look at what's going on for you. Think about what sort of attitude you would like your child to have. If you want them to be a helpful, cheerful and positive person who sees life as a fun challenge, then you need to adopt that worldview as well.

I'm hoping you can understand you are setting an example with everything you do. Your behaviours and attitudes give your child something to look up to and emulate. If your child is acting in a way that suggests they're not getting what they need to feel satisfied, it's worth asking where you might be lacking in terms of feeling understood and happy. Then ask yourself what you are going to do about whatever came up when you answered that question – and do it.

Enjoying looking after yourself

Looking after yourself is as important as looking after your children. Your life is not just about staying safe physically, in terms of food and shelter. It's about a lot more than that. If you have kids who lose the plot all the time, you may find they are mirroring you.

You may consider getting a coach to help you see things differently and guide you to set some goals. You're worth it. This is important because you want to be the role model you would want to have. Imagine a coach who was not giving a hundred percent because they were exhausted. How would that make you feel? Would you want to listen to them?

Nothing is impossible, so don't fret if you're feeling a bit taken aback. Don't suffer in silence but do take a reality check to see what's really going on and needs to be done. Don't hesitate to get whatever help you need to make sure you turn things around. As we've noted, you're always being observed and copied. Keeping your spirits as high as you can, enjoying your life and making the most of it has a great impact on your children and their behaviour.

Meanwhile, there's no question that consistently badly behaved children can really knock the joy out of how you're feeling. Even though you may find it difficult to be on top of the kids for every little misdemeanour, it is necessary for their sake as well as yours to train disrespect out of them and replace it with self-respect and consideration of others.

Have fun

Adding fun gives adults and children a happier life experience in general. You have this wonderful opportunity to relive your own childhood – except this time you get to be the boss. You get to laugh more, play more, sing more, perform more and be silly if you want to because that's the 'job' of kids. Join in. Enjoy the ride.

Our children are teaching us as much as we are teaching them. Join in. See life through your child's eyes and enjoy the ride of your life.

Don't worry if being childlike feels a bit weird at first. I know things will change for you when you start to live in the moment and be more present. You'll also begin to realise that apart from your wonderful family, pretty much everything else is just 'stuff' to be handled.

It's okay to break the rules sometimes

Every human wants to be a rule-breaker sometimes. If your child hates having their hair brushed or doesn't want to do something they know they should do, sometimes you could say: Hey, let's just be naughty today. Let them off the hook. Of course, you can only do this if good behaviour is well entrenched in the child's psyche. It's way too risky to allow for a grey area if kids are still learning how to behave well. When your child sees you are breaking a rule out of love and consideration for their feelings, they will adore you even more for it. This is a very different situation to breaking a rule because you are being manipulated and bullied into doing it by a child who is out of control, bossing you around and thinking they're in charge.

What I know for sure is by giving kids enough reasons to want to be good, you won't have to nag, beg, cry or scream from frustration ever again. When you do break the rules, make sure you tell your children you're doing it as a treat for them because they've been so good. That will make it all the more special. In fact, it might even feel like something they can really treasure and will probably remember when they grow up.

Essentially, you can make anything sound appealing if you say it in the right way. It's all in the delivery. My secret strategy when my kids were young was to finish an instruction with something that sounded urgent, like: Quick. I'm counting. See if you can get back before I count to ten. It is quite lovely to watch my daughter doing this with her 4-year-old now. By having a magic bag full of tricks and treats, you can help your child to have fun and feel that life is good. When life is fun, it's much easier to help kids to see it's worth putting the effort into trying to be their best.

Part of living a well-balanced, enjoyable life is to be kind to each other, to look after ourselves and the people we care about and to push ourselves a little bit further than we may sometimes want to. True wellbeing comes from pushing ourselves a little so we can enjoy family life and still get things done. We must make this a priority. Sometimes we can get stuck in a rut and feel overwhelmed. This sucks the life out of us. A change of attitude can be all you need to manage your family and also have some energy left for self-care. All the stress from challenging behaviours will start to diminish as your confidence and motivation increases.

Don't overcommit

I want you to think about whether you have overcommitted your time and your children's time recently. If so, cut back without delay. Don't worry that your child won't keep up if you cancel a few things. They will do better and feel better if they choose one or two things to do after school, rather than five or six activities, just because their friends are doing them.

Children benefit from unstructured play and time to do just nothing. That gives them a chance to get in some creative play, hang out with their neighbours, help you with the dinner or simply do nothing. Daydreaming, lying around and listening to music, reading a book you love and walking about in nature are all ways to recuperate from our over-structured lives and are also incredibly beneficial for children.

If there's anything you're doing just because you've always done it, ask yourself if you're still getting joy from it. If not, I suggest you just stop. You may disappoint a few people but don't worry, they'll get over it. What you don't want to miss out on is the valuable time creating the home life you deserve. It's the incidental moments where we connect with our children on a daily basis that mean so much.

Enjoy your children

Because children are so in tune with you and your feelings, they are affected by your moods. I'm sure you've noticed that when you are stressed, your children become super annoying. Even if you're doing your best to mask being stressed, they will still know.

It's so important to eliminate as much unnecessary annoying behaviour as humanly possible so you can 'like' as well as 'love' your children. When someone likes who you are, you naturally behave in a better way. This is the same for your children. When you can take that leap, it's like you're suddenly living the opposite of what was a vicious cycle – a loving cycle. I remember visiting my grandparents as a child. I knew they loved and adored me because they genuinely smiled every time they looked at me. They also hugged me a lot. They made me feel really special.

It's wonderful for everyone, young and old, to have someone who makes us feel special. They help us to be better people because we never want to let them down. I promise you that once you get your children being thoughtful and respectful, you will be that same person – leaving your child with no doubt that you have positive regard for them. Their behaviour will then reflect that.

Let your child know who they are

From about the age of 5 or 6, children love to get to know their family history, especially the part about you. You can fill them in by talking about old times. Tell them about your childhood and what your mum and dad used to do. They especially like hearing about how you met your partner. Kids love hearing about times when their parents were naughty and what their parents did to punish them. They want to know what made you laugh and what pets you had – they want to know it all.

At bedtime, you might like start telling your children a story about your life. Then, just as it gets interesting, stop. With your children now intrigued, let them know that if they go straight to sleep you'll tell them the rest of the story tomorrow. If they push you, say playfully: Well, I can't remember. I'll try to remember in time for bedtime tomorrow. Kids love a bit of theatre and the thrill of anticipation.

Finding some family fun, like storytelling at night, and turning it into a habit creates something very special that bonds the family and ends the day with a beautiful moment of connection. Creating family rituals really helps to make everyone feel as though they belong to a fun tribe. Your children will remember these fun times and remind each other of them when they are adults, helping keep the family connection solid.

CHAPTER 7: APPRECIATION

*Let's be grateful for the people who make us happy.
They are the charming gardeners
who make our souls blossom.*
— Marcel Proust

We've all heard the stories of children who grow up getting every toy and gadget known to man. That might be the way it is in your house. I'm not here to judge anyone. What I want to do is get you thinking about some of the other options to keep your children feeling good about being your child in your family.

The problem I see for children who get so many possessions given to them, is they rarely get much pleasure from those possessions. Instead, they get caught up in a vicious cycle with an insatiable need for 'more'. The best gifts you can give your kids are the gifts of gratitude and appreciation. Time and time again, I see children being given so much that it seems to bring out a kind of numbness in them. That might seem an overstatement but there's definitely a lack of appreciation in these poor children who are drowning in material possessions.

I love to experiment with the families I'm called in to help. What I do is take away most of the toys, just leaving a few for the kids to play with each week. What invariably happens is the children become super excited to play with the toys they ignored before because they were hidden under all the new stuff. I've also experimented with taking away toys from 10-month-old children (or thereabouts) and giving them a saucepan and spoon to play with instead. They love it because, from their perspective, their adults play with those things as well. Something to bang on, something that holds water to pour in the bath and a cuddly toy for bed is enough to keep most young children entertained and learning for ages. The trick here is to regularly remove and replace possessions. They will begin to appreciate what they have so much more.

When I look at all the children's toys on the market today, I feel like they're all the same. It's the same plastic, the same gelato colours, the same texture. They really all just blend into a mess on the floor in bedrooms and playrooms. It's the same all over the world. Invariably, there's not enough storage space in most of the homes I go to because kids just have so much stuff. And having stuff everywhere is an incredibly unsettling environment to live in.

I was a bit spoiled because my children went to a Steiner school where they learned that caring for their things was important. The belief is that if we don't care for our things then we tend not to care for people either. I think he's right. It makes me really sad to see so many things and people being taken for granted. So, I'm on a mission to change this and remind families, in particular, that gratitude makes the world go around. Gratitude helps everyone feel happier and more fulfilled. It's certainly an important lesson to teach our children.

It is the best of times ...
— Charles Dickens

I like to start this story with two quotes – the shortened version of a famous quote from Charles Dickens, seen above, and this one:

Feeling Gratitude and not expressing it is like wrapping a present and not giving it.
— William Arthur Ward

I'm hoping the two combined quotes will set the scene for what you are about to experience in the following story.

Did you realise that when someone does something nice for you, or even says a nice thing to you, it gives your brain a little shot of the happiness chemical, 'dopamine'? It was studied by researchers, Kumar and Epley, who wondered about the benefits of gratitude on your wellbeing.

This caused me think about families and the struggles that so many have. So often, every member of the family feels the stresses of everyday life, becoming so overwhelmed at times that 'gratitude' may be the furthest thing from their minds.

I wondered if 'gratitude' would help families to be happier – lets' see what you think.

Yesterday, I made a conscious effort to call a dozen or so families I have worked with in the past. I told them I really appreciated my time spent with their family. I said I often thought of them and wondered how they were doing.

That was all I said but, wow, what a wonderful experience it was for me. It seems you can create your own experiences and opportunities to feel grateful. The best thing I discovered is that it causes a chain reaction of happy feelings.

It's interesting how humans behave. We tend to worry that we'll make a person uncomfortable by telling them we're grateful for something they've done so we avoid doing it – whereas the opposite is true. Letting people know we appreciate them has benefits for everyone.

It's worth our while to work on overcoming our fear of letting others know how much we appreciate them. Why not make it a daily exercise to cultivate gratitude? All it takes is fifteen minutes before bed, writing down your positive emotions, and what you're grateful for, in a 'gratitude journal'. Later, you can share your feelings of gratitude knowing this will not only improve your own wellbeing, but also that of those around you.

Isn't that what's it all about – not the things, but the love?

We can only have a happy life if we are living with awareness and gratitude. Learning this is an important part of a child's development. Teaching kids to notice and appreciate what others are doing for them is the greatest gift you can ever give your child. The more children are made aware of how much we do for them, without having to take on any guilt about it, the more they will start to appreciate the people in their life.

As it is now, children are used to wandering around, making a mess, dropping things, and taking and breaking things without any concept of what goes into providing for them, not to mention cleaning up after them. It doesn't have to be that way. Appreciation, awareness and manners can be taught.

And it's never too early, or too late, to start. With a baby, it's as simple as saying 'Ta' or 'Thank you' when they take something from you. If you are about to start doing this with your first child, you will probably swell up with pride to a point where you almost burst when your child starts to repeat these words back to you without being prompted.

Something as simple as this is an absolutely fabulous foundation for gratitude and appreciation to grow. As the children get older, continually reminding them how to appreciate what you are doing for them, or giving to them, is the best way to reinforce the things they learned when they were little. Even teenagers can be taught to be more conscious and aware by understanding life isn't all about them – it's also about remembering how important the people they love and care for are.

Once you have your children acknowledging and valuing the people who love and care for them, you will notice this foundation of gratitude flows over to other areas of their life. I know that compared to social media and PlayStation games, family and nature can seem boring to kids today. It's a bit of a trick to get some children from wanting a 'like' to wanting a cool breeze on their face while sitting on a hill staring out to sea – but it's essential we make the effort to achieve this. We are committing a crime against the humanity of our kids if we allow them to miss the wonder of nature and how it soothes the soul, heating us when we're cold and playing games on us unexpectedly. Don't let that happen to your children.

Helping our children learn all the beauty the simple things in life and the gifts that nature give us is invaluable. There are so many gorgeous things to revel in every day. Sadly, most people rush through life without even noticing what's going on around them. They're wasting so much precious time inside their busy head or constantly focused on a screen.

As a conscious parent, you can help your child to be aware of the nuances of nature so they don't miss out on the beauty and joy all around them. This is important because the world we live in is so busy and full of noise that demands our attention and unless children are taught how to slow down and really smell the roses, they won't ever know how to do it.

CHAPTER 8: MINDFULNESS

Too often we underestimate the power of a touch, a smile, a kind word, a listening ear, an honest compliment, or the smallest act of caring, all of which have the potential to turn a life around.
— Leo Buscaglia

To me, mindfulness means understanding ourselves, being in the present moment and paying attention. By being more emotionally open with others, we learn more about what's really going on for them. We learn to stop rushing for rushing's sake and we begin to notice a whole lot more. Mindfulness helps us become more stable in terms of our moods and gives us a deeper understanding of what impacts them. This helps us interact well with our partners and our children and helps us notice the inner voice and attitudes towards ourselves.

Helping children to become mindful is a gift. Once your children have learned how to listen happily, you will have more time to teach things that aren't 'urgent' but are morally important. These are aspects a happy family can't live without, such as teaching children how to self-soothe, entertain themselves and other skills that help them grow into contented and thoughtful adults. Being aware of qualities such as thoughtfulness, patience, loyalty and kindness, to name just a few, is how we become self-aware adults. We need to acquire these virtues and many others to live consciously within a family and society.

Being a conscious human is simply a better life. For a start, being thoughtful helps you be a better partner, neighbour, employee or parent. People are drawn to you.

These days the 'important stuff', like virtues, seem to take a backseat to vices. Many people are addicted to myriad things, such as being busy, phones, virtual games, social media and staying inside. These vices spread into other areas of family life over time. While we still have influence, we must show our children what self-control looks like by modelling it ourselves.

Without facing these things, children miss out on enjoying one of the most heart-warming times of their lives – growing up and being involved in your family. Having fun together, laughing and bonding with our people creates authentic relationships and memories you never forget and that's what makes life worth living. The difficulty is that we don't know what we don't know.

Before I jump ahead of myself, let's look at what living with a child is like if they haven't been taught how to think of others. It's going to be hard for everyone. Learning how to love the important people in our lives, and how to act mindfully and responsibly in the family and wider groups we belong to, is more important than learning the plethora of skills parents pay others to teach their children - skills which may possibly be of little or no use to them in the greater scheme of things.

Don't get me wrong, it's great for kids to have opportunities to explore things they love, such as learning an instrument, playing a sport or speaking another language. This may just be the thing that really lights them up inside. But what I'm hoping you'll understand is kids really need to learn, first and foremost, how to behave well and be nice. To do that, kids may need to give up a few of the extracurricular activities they're signed up for so they can have more time to just be.

Making the most of it

These days, everyone's life is so full of 'doing', which can cause anxiety and stress. Even when some things are enjoyable, the constant rushing here and there is not. There is always going to be things to do every day we would prefer not to do. I believe the difference between a contented life, where we get to experience the satisfaction of achieving things that are a stretch for us, and a mediocre life, where we just get by and feel kind of empty, comes down to the attitude we take, in relation to the stuff we would prefer not to have to do.

Attitudes are contagious and, as you know, yours is being observed daily. For this reason, you need to make sure you have a positive attitude your kids can model their attitude on, and therefore be able to enjoy the life you would like them to have. The trick is to notice if you have developed any attitudes or habits that perhaps you're not proud of but have somehow slipped into your life without realising it. Mindfulness gives us the opportunity to notice our behaviours.

I recommend you regularly and actively remember to slow down and take stock. If you feel like you don't even know where to start, you might like to take a look at "Insight Timer" (https://insighttimer.com/) where You'll find beautiful free meditations and short courses. I'm pretty sure these will help you get into a state that makes it easier for you to get out of autopilot and be a more conscious, confident parent. In the meantime, all you need to do is remember that each and every day is a new opportunity to be the kind of parent you wished you had as a child. Each morning is an opportunity to be thought of as 'day one', rather than thinking of 'one day'.

Another behaviour prevalent in Western culture is the inability to quiet our minds and to *slow down* so we can observe and respond to what's actually happening in our lives, instead of reacting or overreacting and ultimately feeling bad about ourselves. We must find the time to slow down so we're able to communicate lovingly from our hearts without stress. It's only then that we can really be there for our partner and children and see how the rest of our family is really feeling about themselves, their lives and how they are doing.

Relationships take time. The time you put into your relationships will actually pay you back many times over, especially when it comes to your family. It's so important to get this right. Managing relationships is way more important than the other things we tend to keep ourselves busy with, such as social media, unnecessary worrying and over-organising. Once you eliminate these time-consuming activities and stop worrying about things that haven't happened yet, and probably never will, then you'll have more energy and space to relax, rejuvenate, reconnect and really enjoy life.

No need to be perfect

Perfectionism is one of the main culprits, when it comes to having time to relax and maintain our energy. If you feel as though you fuss too much and create more work for yourself than necessary, there are some really simple steps you can take to eliminate that.

Begin with the obvious things like cooking three separate meals for dinner, instead of one. This not only eats into your time but also creates fussy eaters for life and children who feel special for being difficult. Ask yourself where else you could be toughening up and cutting back on wasting energy? Are you constantly cleaning the house until it's perfect? Are you overcommitting your child so you're always having to arrange and organise? Could certain clothes just be hung up and thus available for another wear? Do you iron clothing that could make do with a good shake?

All that unnecessary 'doing' doesn't make anyone happier; it just makes everyone busier. To sum up, I want you to get off the hamster wheel of life, take stock, cut back where you can and relax a whole lot more. This way, you make better decisions about what's most important to you and your unique beautiful family.

When we *slow down*, we get to notice more and see what's really going on. We are then able to make better choices. Let go of having that perfect life – who cares; it's not possible anyway – and free yourself up to embrace a relaxed, happier life for you and your family. Making time to spend with your family – playing, laughing and mucking about – is what real connection with each other is all about. By removing the stress generated by rushing around every day, you actually give your children many more advantages than they would get from being constantly organised. You are creating an environment where your children can develop true self-worth because they know they matter more than anything to you. Best of all, you'll find they are calmer and happier because of that.

Sharing child-focused time playing with your children and having fun together has many benefits because it's the physical contact we all need. Roll around the floor, piggy back, toe count – whatever gets everyone laughing and being playful as a family.

Keep it lighthearted if you can

It goes without saying that adding lightheartedness into the family dynamic will give you and the children a happier day-to-day experience. The beauty of children is they help you see life through different eyes. We get to laugh more, play more, sing more and be silly because that's what being a child is all about. I read once that it's never too late to have a happy childhood.

We learn as much from our kids as they learn from us as parents. There's nothing better than remembering how enjoyable it is to learn new things and to have fun again. Any day you choose, you can make a decision to start to live in the moment. Being in the present, experiencing playfulness and thoughtfulness, is what having a family is all about – the rest of it is *'just more stuff'* you can handle as needed. Knowing this took a huge weight off my shoulders, leaving room to feel freer and more creative which, by the way, is what all children of any age naturally want.

Change your self-talk, change your life

It's the simple things that make a difference – like judging your thoughts and changing them.

I used to always say 'I have to …'. When I changed it to 'I get to …', I suddenly started looking forward to more things.

Don't neglect self-care

Remember that before you were a parent, you were a person. And you still are. If you're not allowing that person to shine and you don't remember to be who you really are, then you risk losing yourself to parenting. At the very least, your energy is likely to be depleted. Being depleted will make it all but impossible for you to be able to teach your children how to have a full life of happiness and authentic living. Now could be a good time to ask yourself a potentially uncomfortable question:

> *Am I happy or have I lost my joy somewhere along the way?*

Please don't worry if you find you don't like your answer. You've already started to free yourself by the ground we've covered already.

Disrupting existing patterns of behaviour within the family

This is a huge topic and yet it's as easy as just noticing what is going on and wondering if it's how you like it – or if you'd like to explore another way.

I am an observer of others – particularly of how families relate to each other. A friend of mine has a teenage son who never listens to her when she speaks to him. He gets away with that and other unacceptable behaviour, such as stealing from her and lying to her. She has managed to brush it off with a one-liner:

That's teenagers for you.

It's a problem so immense, I don't think she can 'go there' so she tries to convince herself it's a normal part of development.

For some it is and for those children it's up to the parents to ensure the child knows, in no uncertain terms, that it has to stop.

Grab some 'me' time everyday

Sometimes all you need is some alone time. You may like to take a long bath, lash out and have a massage or take a mini break away from responsibilities. It's important to ensure that, at the very least, you have regular time out for yourself to calm your mind. This is not only good for you but it will also be good for your family.

I say this because that little bit of 'me time' will result in you staying well and will also teach your children how important it is for them to take time out to look after themselves as they need it. You will show them you are an individual as well as their parent. The aim here is to remind yourself and your children that your life is not all about them. Your children may well be the most important things in your life but they are not the only things. You and your partner should also have guilt-free time without the children as often as you can manage. Go for dinners and holidays so that, as a couple, you remember to nurture that connection. I have seen many families destroyed because mum and dad were too busy being mum and dad and forgot to be loving partners.

It's interesting to think about the gift that the COVID pandemic brought along with the problems it presented. In Australia, the first major consequence was the government lockdown. This meant that adults had time they hadn't had before – time they would normally have spent travelling to and from work or taking the children to and from school. Some parents seemed to fill their extra time on screens but others really got involved in doing great home-schooling, cooking together, being really creative and just having fun with their children.

Pandemic or no pandemic, what I want you to do is make sure you reward yourself by doing something you love – every day. Take a walk, go for a cycle, sit down to meditate, get out into nature – whatever works for you. It's so important you make the time to do something for yourself. You might need to *wake up* and get out of the house at 5.30 am to take your daily walk but once you get into that habit, you'll find it's actually a beautiful time of day. That was my daily exercise for years. Summer, winter, wet or dark, my friend would collect me at my home and we would head out to the Bay Run – which we walked – and had heaps of time to gab and giggle. I loved it. If that doesn't work for you, though, then it might be 7.30 at night while your partner puts the kids to bed and loads the dishwasher. Taking time for yourself will make you a more relaxed and a happier person to live with, not to mention being a much better parent.

You may also be surprised to find, once you let go of the reins, your partner is very capable of doing things – you know, the 'things' you thought were quicker and easier if you just did them. Mums, in particular, need to try to focus more on what their partners can do and less on what they think they could do better. We all like to know we are doing a great job but if you criticise someone often enough they'll probably just check out and even begin to resent you a little. This is another hidden blind spot neither of you may notice until it's too late, so keep an eye on that. It may be time to notice if criticism or something similarly ungracious is happening in your family. You could even be wondering why you get stuck with all the work at home. Some things in our lives are seen so clearly by others but, for some reason, they are blind spots to us. Mindfulness is helpful to start gaining more awareness

Below are some timesavers you could implement to create more spare time, allowing you to spend more quality time together with the people you love.

- Give everyone some extra daily chores and explain why at your family meeting. You can even get your kids to inspect each other's work.
- Cook less by making a couple of dishes a week that will work for a second night's dinner.
- Don't cook to everyone's desires – one simple nutritious meal is always enough.
- Fold the washing as it comes off the line or out of the dryer and put it straight into the cupboards to eliminate having full washing baskets.

- Iron nothing except clothes that really need it – usually only work clothes.
- Ask other parents to babysit while you have a date night at least once a month. Keeping your relationship happy does wonders for the family dynamics. You can repay the favour by having their kids for a sleepover or even going over and watching Netflix at their house.

What if I don't feel like it?

You are not superhuman. There's nothing whatsoever wrong with you if some days you don't feel particularly enthusiastic. No-one is even going to notice if you aren't the so-called perfect parent every day. Try not to be 'down' for too long, though, because it really does affect the children if you are.

Sometimes faking it before you make it is an excellent strategy to get out of 'worrying about something' or 'an annoying mood'. If you force yourself to smile, laugh and act happy, then you may just find there's something to be happy about. It's great how that can work. Give it a try and crack a smile or even a joke, even if you don't feel like it. By squeezing the muscles in your cheeks, like we do when we smile, your body will send some endorphins your way. So, in a sense, when you smile on the outside, you're going to eventually find you're smiling on the inside too. Ten or twenty star jumps while looking up at the sky is a proven mood enhancer and one I have used for myself, my staff and my children many times to shift stale energy.

Your child has moods too. In fact, teenagers are famous for them. But just like us, they don't have to be ruled by them, unless they've been diagnosed with a disorder and need medication. It's incredibly important for you to teach your children how to be happy, especially if they have gotten into a habit of being sulky or rude.

Hopefully, you've kept the lines of communication open and have addressed any issue your moody kid could be affected by before trying to snap them out of it. I'm pointing out that sometimes, as I previously said, moods can just be a habit that no-one noticed as it formed. Bad moods affect everyone in the home and they're hard to live with. Starting a better-quality habit begins with recognising what's going on first.

Have a positive outlook

It's incredibly important to have an outlook that totally supports and embraces the changes you're wanting to bring about in your family. Fundamental to your attitude is your perception of what things are or what's going on. We all see things differently but the way we perceive things often changes. In my case, it can be something as simple as hearing someone else's perspective of a situation. This applies to being able to look at adversity or difficulties in a different way than how you currently are. Often a positive attitude to a crappy situation has a roll-on effect, giving us opportunities we otherwise could have missed out on.

You may meet someone who benefits your life, be offered a work opportunity or see possibilities that help you grow without even realising the adversity you experienced created that. For example, I recently had to suddenly leave my accommodation and move into a huge house with others. I wasn't thrilled with the arrangement but it turned out that a person I would never have met otherwise was instrumental in getting this book edited and published. So there you go – you never know. If I had been sulky and moody about my situation, this opportunity may never have come about.

I have had many seemingly disastrous situations turn around because my positive outlook gave me opportunities for future growth, rather than seeing something difficult as stopping me from being happy and living the life I wanted to live. This is one of the most valuable things you could ever teach your children. Being positive will set them up to be far more resilient with whatever life throws at them, as well as making it more enjoyable for your children and the people around them.

This is the attitude good leaders have. Unfortunate things happen all the time but great leaders don't let unfortunate things take away their joy. They move on and grow stronger through adversity. Wouldn't you like your children to have an attitude like this, too? It's up to the parent to show their children how to focus on the positives in life. Your relationship with your children means everything to them. Showing them how to live with gratitude and mindfulness helps them to grow up with a positive outlook. We all know there's nothing worse than living in fear or having a negative attitude towards life.

When we take a moment to consider why some children are well-behaved, happy and well-mannered while others are always complaining and looking downright miserable, we wonder if this was inevitable? Were these kids just born that way? Are they simply going through a difficult phase? Is that just the way they are? I think not. Sure, we all come into the world with different temperaments but what I see in the way children behave now is about a lot more than temperament. Moodiness and bossy behaviour is the net effect of every little thing they have learned and been able to get away with on a daily basis.

Problematic behaviour only grows and develops when parents enable it by not stopping poor attitudes and actions before they become a habit. I fully believe if parents nipped bad behaviour and moodiness in the bud the minute kids tried it on, it would never become a habit. Really understanding this is the launchpad to creating a better future for your children. Once we see the truth, and *wake up*, we can change things for the better. If we can't see the truth, however, we have no hope.

To the best of my ability, I want to help mums and dads know exactly what they can do to have the relationship and connection they need to be the family leaders their children respect and love. Parenting based on guilt, ego, pride or denial – especially when it comes to identifying things that aren't working – has to be a thing of the past so families can avoid struggling so much.

There's a whole industry out there promoting personal development that encourages leadership and strength, while the parenting industry encourages the opposite. More than ever before, parents seem to be trying to position themselves as their children's friends. The problem with doing this is your children don't need friends your age. What they need is strong, loving and committed parents to teach them how to get on in the world they've been born into. That's not a friend's job. Of course, parents should be friendly but children need a strong, loving leader and manager first. Someone has to lead the tribe, even children know that. If you don't step up, they will.

However, they will never thank you for handing over your authority – nor will they respect you for it.

Being mindful means you realise it's no longer okay to hope and pray things will just get better over time. Doing whatever it takes, even when we don't feel like it, is the only option to create the changes needed if we've allowed damaging behaviours or bad attitudes to seep into our families.

If you were born to parents who you felt could have tried harder to be better parents, then I bet they didn't have the parents they really wanted either. Now it's up to you to break the family cycle and be the parent you wish you had.

PART 3

Getting your kids to play BALL

CHAPTER 9: BOUNDARIES

Walls keep everybody out. Boundaries teach people where the door is.
— Mark Groves

When you see someone in a happy and healthy relationship, it's a fair bet they have healthy boundaries in place. Having a lack of boundaries, or poorly defined ones, is often behind the problems faced by people who contact me for help. Once I start asking parents a few questions, it doesn't take too long for the truth to emerge with statements like: We can't get the children to do what we ask them to do. And here lies the number one problem – often when you ask a child to do something, they think that 'ask' means optional. The bottom line is that boundaries are absolutely critical. Knowing how to enforce them helps get struggling families back on track.

Among other things, the section in Chapter 3 about establishing rules gave you the foundation on which to make decisions about the boundaries you need

CHAPTER 9: BOUNDARIES

to put in place. Now we can cover the critical skills needed to make sure the boundaries are respected.

Getting everyone to understand and buy into the rules that underpin boundaries may not happen overnight. However, if you have weekly meetings, where communication can flow freely and ideas are flagged, you'll have a platform to reiterate and reinforce the rules around family boundaries on an ongoing basis without having to repeat yourself all day long.

You could even use the weekly meetings to congratulate family members who you've seen making great decisions about protecting their own boundaries or respecting the boundaries of others. Having boundaries helps us know what is expected of us in society, as well as in the home. That sounds simple enough, I know, but consistently maintaining boundaries is where parents often let the team down.

Human nature is geared to seek what we like and avoid what we don't. That's why the concept of playing BALL is so important for families. If you can teach children about boundaries with a touch of fun, but still be firm about keeping to the rules, your children will see having boundaries is not such a bad thing. In fact, if you set boundaries up well they will give your children a sense of certainty around how the family works and prepare them to be able to have other healthy relationships well beyond their immediate family.

Children want to learn as much as they can as quickly as possible, and this includes learning what is expected of them. Without a doubt, pushing boundaries and experiencing the consequences of stepping into territory they are not ready for is part of growing up. However, it's up to us as parents to guide and teach our children exactly where their boundaries within the family lie. Once that's determined, we can then move the boundaries as soon as our kids are ready. Remember, knowing how to 'be good', gives children a sense of being capable. If we allow out-of-control behaviour, then our kids will think of themselves as 'out-of-control'.

Way too many parents incorrectly believe that overloading children with toys, excusing their rudeness and giving in to them will make them feel happy and loved. We just need to take a look around to see this is not the case. When children are moody and act out, hitting or yelling at the people around them, they are not happy. Happy children are respectful and grateful.

Being attentive to your child's needs – being family conscious – will enable you to tap into your common sense, innate wisdom or whatever parents draw on to know when boundaries need to be moved.

Needless to say, it won't always be when and where your children think that they should. It may sound tough but children are masters at manipulation. How sophisticated their manipulative strategies are will depend on their age and the extent to which they've been able to get away with convincing you to do things their way. Here is how situations can pan out if you've been used to caving in to your child demands.

Scenario 1

Your child wants you to buy them something at the supermarket. You say no and they throw a tantrum, screaming in the middle of the shop. This draws the attention of everyone in the vicinity.

Option 1

Give them what they want to keep them quiet, therefore reinforcing their behaviour. Assure yourself you'll address this later with a stern conversation.

Option 2

Try to redirect their attention as they carry on but hold your ground. Tell them, in no uncertain terms, there is absolutely no point in continuing. Keep shopping. Pretend to be consumed in deciding what you want to buy. When they settle down a bit, ask if they have finished in a bland tone. Take their hand and say: Well done. Keep walking. Suggest something you can do together when you're out of the supermarket to refocus their thoughts.

Scenario 2

You need your child to get ready quickly so you can get out the door on time. They're playing with Lego and are completely consumed in the game and not interested in your agenda. They pretend not to hear you.

Option 1

After calling out that it's time to leave two or three times, you then scream at him and drag him out of the room. You feel frustrated. He bursts into tears.

Option 2

You touch them on the shoulder, say their name and ask them to look at you. When you have eye contact, you ask them to stand up and say: Come on, we're leaving now. Quick, off we go. Grab their hand and help them walk out the door with you nicely. If they refuse, you calmly pack the Lego up and tell them you will be confiscating it for 24 hours (or whatever disincentive you decide to put in place). Your job is to encourage your children to get up and get ready when they are asked to.

Scenario 3

The child is making loud and irritating noises while you're driving. Each time you ask them to stop, they begin again a minute or so later. You finally get to the point where you start screaming at them, and both of you get really upset.

Option 1

Keep doing what you're doing and acclimatise the child to being screamed at so this becomes a useless deterrent.

Option 2

Stop the car. Turn around and say: Because you have no control over yourself, the new car rule is no-one can talk in the car except me. Do you understand?

You'll probably get complete silence. Keep asking until they say: Yes, I understand.

Keep looking at them and ask firmly: Are you sure?

They'll probably nod their head. Tell them: Great. Now, just look out the window, until we get there.

Once silence is established, you could put on the radio. Tell your child they can sing along with the music if they can control themselves, or you can simply put on a classical station which is good ambiance for silence. If your child starts up with the loud noises again, send them to their room as soon as you get home. There, they'll be allowed to do nothing or read a book of your choice. If they are too young to read, say they can look through their books, but no playing. This is time for them to think about controlling themselves.

Scenario 4

Your child is crawling all over you whining, pushing you and slapping you to gain your attention while you're speaking to someone on the phone. You ask them to stop but they just keep going.

Option 1

You scream at them and try to push them off. Their mission to get your attention is achieved. You've lost the power and wound up angry and frustrated. Be assured, this behaviour will definitely happen again.

Option 2

You say: I'm busy now – just wait. Or tell them to stop. If they still don't listen, stand up and walk into another room, closing the door behind you. There's likely to be a lot of screaming and possibly kicking of the door. As long as the child is safe, all you need to do is hold your nerve. This way you maintain the power and they learn this kind of behaviour is not going to get them what they want, in this case, your attention. When everything settles down, tell them exactly what they need to do next time and let them know that if this happens again, you'll be walking away again and you'll be putting them in their room to think about their behaviour. The timeframe spent in their room depends on their age but you'll be able to work that out. Do not call them by any endearing names. Look bored. Sound firm.

The list of challenging behaviours children might pull out of the bag is almost endless. The thing to remember when you're going through any of these issues is your child is not a bad person, you just haven't found ways that work to make them want to be good – yet. Certainly, their behaviour is less than ideal but from today they will be learning better ways to get what they want. What happens when you stand in your power and play the long game, rather than caving in and letting them get away with blue murder, is what you can discover and experience very soon.

What we're going to do now is take a snapshot of how things are playing out in your current family dynamic.

Table 1

Do your children:	Yes	No
rudely answer back?		
ignore you?		
lack respect?		
complain a lot?		
get bored easily?		

If you have any ticks in the 'yes' column in the table above, then you have some work to do. Stay committed to your outcomes and you will be amazed at how quickly the children respond positively. Even getting bored easily is a behaviour that needs to change because learning to entertain ourselves is a must if we want to enjoy life. Kids need to learn this skill.

Table 2

Do your children:	Yes	No
greet you when you get home?		
look at you when they say 'hi' and 'bye'?		
help you around the house?		
clean up after themselves?		
unpack their school bags and put their things away?		

Hopefully, they are all 'yes' responses. There are real bonuses to good behaviour. Children with positive traits are 'seen' by others, including teachers, who are willing to spend more time helping your child. Other parents will be keen to invite your child over for playdates. And your kids will also attract friends who share similar traits. Everyone wins. Wonderful attributes, such as optimism, curiosity, self-control, zest, social intelligence, gratitude and my favourite, good manners, can all be taught.

I don't want you to worry if you don't like the results you got from this simple exercise, just remember that awareness is power. You are now in a powerful position to help your children turn unhelpful behaviours into more enriching and resourceful ones. Discovering what's really going on means you now won't ignore the little things you know you can take control of, even if they previously seemed too hard to deal with or didn't really matter. Each minor moment of disrespect can seem insignificant but these moments add up, causing you to lose a little more respect each time. And remember, children only listen to people they respect or fear. Let's always ensure that respect is the motivator in your family.

To determine the motivation behind your child's behaviour, think about whether your child is:

- wanting a hug for affection or is just trying to annoy and manipulate you because they're bored and you're busy
- crying because they've hurt themselves or something is actually making them sad, or because they're manipulating you or just want to be annoying
- refusing vegetables because they aren't hungry or because they want something sweet

- going to the bathroom every hour because they have a stomach bug or because they're sneaking in to check social media
- making a valid argument about something or is just arguing in the hope they'll get one over you.

A family I worked with years ago had two lovely well-behaved children – or so it seemed. After a couple of days, the cracks began to show and it became apparent that over-parenting had turned them into unreasonable, entitled kids. Sadly, the parents had fallen into the trap of wanting the children to feel satisfied with every decision they made – where to go, what to eat, wear or watch, when to go to bed or when to have some entertainment. Their parents' agenda or needs never came into the equation. Needless to say, the 7-year-old in this family was a bit taken aback when I first said no to him but he soon realised that with me, he couldn't always get whatever he wanted by challenging me like he did with his parents and he soon began to accept what was happening without argument.

Funnily enough, these parents seemed to believe their children respected them, even against all actions to the contrary, believing they were giving their children every opportunity to develop their intelligence and decisiveness. From my perspective and emotional distance from the situation, I could see what was actually happening was the children were doing what all spoiled children do – taking the parents on, acting out, getting their own way and winning every battle.

This behaviour had been encouraged over the years, so these well-behaved, reasonable children by day, turned into whiny, needy, bossy kids as soon as the parents arrived home. It seemed like the parents had some kind of weird psycho drama playing out, believing they were raising geniuses instead of entitled, moody and bossy kids. This delusion was how these otherwise rational people seemed to interpret their children's manipulative, selfish behaviours as love and respect. I see this common dysfunctional behaviour in so many families today that I despair about the future. These children will be constantly argumentative, wondering what is wrong with everyone. The parents will wonder why their children don't want to listen to them or spend time with them. They'll wonder where they went wrong. I'm hoping we can break this cycle.

As a Nanny, I was skilled at quickly and easily helping children become more conscious of their behaviours and was able to change bad behaviours for nice ones in no time. However, I was not able to make a huge difference for the family in the long term if the mums and dads believed that disrespect and bossing parents around was a normal developmental stage of childhood, so continually caved in to their children.

It was such a shame to witness because many of the destructive behaviours the parents accepted have negative and avoidable long-term repercussions, including destroying marriages sooner or later. If the parents were both being firm, calm and aware, they would have had more time to bond and connect within a loving, respectful family environment.

Over the decades I've worked with families as a Family Coach to create harmony and stability in the home, I've found that allowing children aged between 1 and 7 to have a say in decisions around how the family runs just creates argumentative children. Fortunately, because these parents are ready to change and are more open to finding out why things are hard, they are able to listen and to hear a different perspective.

When parents believe that allowing their children to be challenging helps them to develop confidence – one of the most common of misconceptions – then this is often the foundation of all the problems they're wrestling with in their children.

A loving, happy, respectful family is only possible when the kids are confident their parents know exactly what they are doing. Then, all they need to do is listen and learn. The parents must lead and the children follow – at least until kids are around 14 to 16 years old. This is most important in their children's formative years.

Without any sense of judgement or blame, what I want you to do now is pause for a moment and think about what destructive behaviours may be going on in your family. If you get into the habit of noticing and questioning things that aren't giving you the results you would like to see, then you'll be open to changing the dynamics and getting the results you hope for. It's important we do this work because the ideal state for any family to thrive in is only possible when everyone knows what's expected of them, who the leader is and how to happily stay inside the boundaries.

This is important, because falling for your child's tricks to get their own way only reinforces poor behaviour which makes being a parent harder than it needs to be. Many parents are avoidably stressed and many kids are not gaining the necessary skills they need to get on in life. Taking a 'no' happily and pushing through when we don't want to, helps kids learn resilience. Without resilience, life is overwhelming and can lead to problems with mental health.

Keep things consistent

Most children thrive on routine. Knowing what is going to be happening every day, and what is expected of them, gives children less to worry about. You will see a dramatic improvement in the behaviour of both sensitive children and the wilful ones when they have a clear understanding of what's going on. To the best of your ability, eliminate surprises but help your child to be aware unexpected things happen to all of us sometimes.

Teaching your children how to deal with change is also important. We all need to learn how to cope with things we haven't planned for. It's much easier to manage unexpected situations once we have solid coping foundations in place. That's why keeping the lines of communication open and helping our children learn how to express themselves and trust us with their feelings is imperative.

Teaching your kids this is an incredible bonus to your child's overall wellbeing and to their ability to be more comfortable with uncertainty and difficulties. For this to happen, a child needs to feel loved and understood and they need to know you will always be there for them. Try your best not to fob little things off as unimportant if they are important to your child. Sometimes all we need to do is just listen and nod or hug.

It's a balancing act to get this right, so don't be too hard on yourself if you find you veer too far one way or the other. I would always overreact if someone hurt my child's feelings, though, with hindsight, I later realised that asking the children what they think they should do when things go haywire was a much better way to help them to learn and feel capable.

Life is full of the unexpected and if you approach life with an open mind, your children will be likely to follow your lead. What's more, you might just have some fun laughing at a difficult situation and thus bond with them even more deeply in the process.

You can help your children develop confidence in their abilities by saying positive things like 'You've got this' or 'You can do this' or 'I noticed you're getting so much better at ...' Never forget your children really want you to notice. They love it when you have genuine faith in their abilities.

There are numerous roadblocks that stop you, as parents, from doing what needs to be done. You might be:

- tired
- stressed
- overwhelmed
- confused about what you should do due to too many different pieces of advice
- afraid of making it worse, causing further upset or hurting feelings
- worried about a million things, including getting yelled at
- feeling like you can't be bothered
- feeling sorry for your child for any one of a million reasons
- afraid of confrontation

- over it and just want it to run its course
- hoping the kids will work it out
- used to ignoring it.

Noting what these things are is the beginning of changing your mind about what needs to be done.

Keep a check on the messages you're sending

Not surprisingly, the question of communication intersects with that of boundaries. For example, it's important not to say kind and loving things while you're disciplining your child. This will confuse them about what boundaries they've crossed. For example, don't explain why you're punishing them for swearing at you then end the disciplining conversation with a compliment such as: You're amazing, darling, you really are – I just don't know why you behave that way. If you do that, you breach the boundary you're trying to create and your attempt to instil respect will only confuse them. All they have heard is: You're amazing darling! There are plenty of opportunities during each day for praise – just not at these times.

Finding the right amount of affection and discipline is a balancing act you will have to adjust for each child and situation. Some children will smarten up with just a sideways glance from you, while others will constantly need to hear a firm voice and see the stern face before they even notice there's a problem with what they just did.

It goes without saying that reprimanding your child for being rude or disrespectful calls for a very different approach to the one you would use if they made a mistake. A mistake can be addressed with understanding and nice words because your child is not intentionally trying to challenge anything or anyone – they are just being human. However, if they are refusing to do what you ask them to do, or show any lack of respect at all, you need to make it absolutely clear their behaviour is not appropriate and will not be tolerated in your family. Let them know that even if other children are rude and mean, that's not who 'we are'.

The take-home message here is that you will be shooting yourself in the foot if you are being sympathetic or making excuses for children who are doing the wrong thing. If you find yourself in the position where you need to reset your child's behaviour, you could begin by having a conversation that goes a little bit like this:

> *We love you so much that we stopped helping you to grow when we let you get away with being rude to us and out of control. You know when you did [behaviour] and*

[behaviour], we didn't point out you'd crossed the line. We just ignored it, thinking it would stop but it got worse. We just won't be letting you continue to push the boundaries because it's really upsetting and annoying for the family. We'll be much clearer with you about what's acceptable behaviour and what's not from now on so you aren't confused, okay? Do you understand?

Get your child to acknowledge what you said and then go on to explain what will happen if they continue upsetting the status quo. If you like, you can have fun with role-playing 'how we'll be behaving now'.

I think you'll be pleased with how well your child starts listening to you once you begin to expect them to. When you make it obvious you are making decisions that affect the whole family, and will not tolerate their bad behaviour anymore, you will see a new level of understanding about how their behaviours affect everyone. Basically, you're beginning to raise your child to operate from their higher selves, teaching them how to be their best. What a gift that is for them – and the family.

It's human nature to admire people who have higher standards and your tolerance of bad behaviour can be seen, even subconsciously, as a lack of self-respect.

No-one wants to learn from people we can manipulate, disrespect or ignore. Strong people are those who have boundaries and are not afraid to assert their right to have them respected. If that has eluded you, then from today you can choose to be that strong person your children need and choose to be someone who doesn't allow any form of disrespect from anyone, least of all a child.

There are other unacceptable behaviours you can also nip in the bud, such as being talked over, ignored, dragged on, whacked and so on; none of this helps your child feel better. Neither does it help you feel like a parent who has the confidence to teach your child how to behave nicely. It all just becomes unnecessarily hard work for you and for them. From today, insist all bad behaviour stops so you can enjoy being together, creating stronger bonds through every stage of your child's development.

CHAPTER 10: AWARENESS

Awareness is like the sun. When it shines on things, they are transformed.
— Thich Nhat Hanh

Self-awareness is important when it comes to being a great parent. The only problem is that we live in a world full of distractions that can take us away from who we really are and how authentically we express that.

Taking time to do nothing is important and is often what's needed for you to be open to notice what is really going on in your family and in your life in general. Time out for mum and dad is essential. It's only then we can find the headspace to *question ourselves* to see if we really are happy with the way things are panning out. If you have been one of those families who has every spare moment filled in, without allowing time to just 'be' together, you will miss out on a lot of possibilities and insights. As each of your children go through the various stages of development, it's important you keep an eye on where they are at and what needs to be handled.

I would be very surprised if your children never go through a stage where they want to be in charge. They can be pretty determined to break you down when they're at that stage. It's vitally important to notice and see things for what they really are and constantly be on top of your game. This way, you will see the signs as they emerge.

You may need to begin reminding your child 'how to behave nicely'. Notice every time and realise if your children have developed rude behaviours that you're just ignoring because you don't want to be battling with them every time you see them. Or you may have carelessly become susceptible to their attempts to hoodwink you into allowing them to adopt behaviours you really don't find contribute to family life in a positive way.

Ask yourself these questions:

- Has your child replaced all family time with their constant need to be on their phone?
- Is one child disrespectful to another child?
- Are two of your children ganging up against another?
- Is 'please' and 'thank you' a thing of the past?
- Are you being bossed around and not considered or respected?
- Are you being told you're 'silly' or 'wrong' a lot?

It's important to be on top of these nuances because the one-off remark and a habit are not too far apart from each other. No matter how beguiling or convincing your child might be, don't allow your child to think their behaviour's okay. It's only when you actively notice and stop these things before they become damaging habits that your children learn.

As the parent, teacher and leader, one of your most important jobs is to help everyone stay on track and grounded and to avoid developing any habits that will not help them to be the person they can be.

One of the most mental health and family-damaging common behaviours today, as you already know, is the amount and type of technology children and adults are on.

To modify this, anything that will get you or them out of the house or office and into the fresh air is going to be a start. This is simple and doable for everyone. We all know when you change your environment and get outdoors, you're more able to see things a little differently. Walking, swimming, riding a bike or just being out in nature can all make a tremendous difference to your mood, your level of awareness and your wellbeing. Take every possible opportunity to enjoy these activities together – device free – and see how much more joyous and fulfilled you feel as a family.

Keep your mind active with positive things by learning something new or getting better at something you love. You might like to do a short course on anything from mindfulness to horticulture. It's really fun learning a language and planning holidays together – practising saying hello and goodbye in another language while you're hanging out together at home can be a hoot.

Finding the tiny daily habits and rituals that can make family time fun, or at least lighthearted, is necessary if you want your kids to choose you over a screen. Be creative. Remember, it's the small things that count. Encouraging everyone in the family to follow a daily practice of meditation creates a break from thinking and doing all the time. Meditation, once it becomes a daily ritual, helps with all manner of malaise, not in the least our mental health. Creating a beautiful, designated space with incense, candles and a bright cloth can be encouraging for kids to want to 'be' there, especially if you say it's your special space.

As adults, we all have internal blockages of one kind or other. These can often show up, plunging us back into old behaviours that are not really helpful, and preventing us from creating the positive change we crave.

Once you're an adult human, your brain prefers you stay just the way you are, no matter how difficult your current state might be. Homeostasis is a way our brain works to keep us alive but we can break through the barriers if we just keep remembering how important it is to be our best for our children. We owe it to ourselves and our kids not to give in to destructive habits or addictions.

The thing is that we don't just need to survive as a parent. We love our children more than anything but that is just the beginning – it's actually all the ways we 'show up' that affects who they become. It's hard sometimes when we really just want to do something for ourselves. When you have children, that 'something' needs to be considered more carefully.

Aiming to parent with a high level of awareness so we can raise well rounded and resourceful children, with as few childhood issues as possible, has to be the goal. Sometimes we need help. I really encourage you, if you're able, to tap into the wealth of experience that your parents, grandparents and in-laws can bring to the table. Having a loving, extended family can be so comforting and helpful to you and your children and it's worth investing time into building on those relationships. I had a mother-in-law who changed my life. She gave me unconditional love, advice, time and care, and she taught me a lot about life and being a wife. She even took the time to listen to me for hours as I tried to learn the piano. I bet your extended families will be more than willing to share whatever they know with you and give you their time. You may have to open the channels for them to feel as though they are not treading on anyone's toes. Your parents and in-laws may not have been perfect parents but they do have the benefit of hindsight and maturity. They can fill you in on what they would do differently if they had their time over, and what worked brilliantly for them when they were dealing with the kinds of things you are dealing with now.

Yvonne Lavine, author of *Sweet 16: What advice would you give your 16 year old self?*, says:

> *There may be confusion, sadness, joy, clarity or even resentment lingering. But also there is compassion and a recognition in the journey we call life, that binds us all ... and the sharing of our intergenerational stories, there is a great opportunity for healing and learning for the storyteller and the listener.*

It makes me incredibly sad to think that our wise elders, who may not have the vast knowledge that Google has, still have valuable wisdom and experience that Google doesn't have are being ignored. The grandparents of our children will take their wisdom to the grave with them. This is happening basically because the potential beneficiaries of their knowledge are too busy, angry or proud to ask for help or take the time to listen. Generations of your ancestors' stories and advice could be lost forever as a result. Most importantly, these people love you and your children and want the best for you. They are worth respecting and listening to. When you think about it, it's really only Western cultures who don't value their elders.

If you have an extended family who cares about you and your children, please don't overlook their importance.

Emotion regulation

All of us feel like lashing out sometimes but this is generally not an acceptable response. We must learn self-control and the sooner the better. Teaching our children how to deal with their emotions without lashing out is an important lesson and one which some have never been taught. If children see their parents lashing out, so will they. Don't worry if that's a habit you've formed – just apologise, be authentic, tell your children it's not nice and it's no longer going to be how you express your feelings.

Children love it when parents apologise. They never hold it against you but they do remember to mention it a lot when they grow up – grrr.

It's not only children who have triggers, we all do. Learning what these triggers are, and how to keep our dignity when they flare up, is an important life skill and often easier if taught young, but it's never too late to learn.

Sadly, for many parents, anyone saying anything less than complimentary about our children or parenting will trigger us. Yes that was me, especially when these comments came from relatives. Remember, if you can move on from such responses and learn not to overreact or take offence easily you can then start to develop a family support TEAM who love you and your children, and who will be there to help you when things get hard.

So many families stop talking to each other because someone made a throwaway comment or attempted to help you parent better. Wham! That's the end of that relationship. We must get tougher skin if we are to have the family support we sometimes need.

It's important not to let our tendency to be defensive block us from being able to hear what we need to hear. No-one wants to hear what they don't want to hear – but it's usually what we need to hear.

As the parent, it's our responsibility to know what our own triggers are, as well as those of our children. The only way we can help our children understand how to be conscious and self-aware kids and adults, is by pointing out their triggers and working on them together. Again, this is another sometimes difficult conversation but once you break through the defensiveness, there is gold at the other end. When you start teaching your children how to breathe through their uncomfortable feelings and notice that they pass pretty quickly, this is something useful they can draw on even when you are not around.

Vanessa, my favourite person in the whole world then and now, was not even one year old when I realised she hated people laughing at her. In fact, she still does. It's so funny to notice that her son, my brilliant and special grandson, has exactly the same response if someone laughs at him. I'm sharing this with you to acknowledge that even a parent who is as self-aware and switched on as my daughter failed to notice this was one of her son's triggers until someone (her husband) pointed it out. Sometimes, as parents, we are too close to the 'problem' to be able to see what it is. Having a blind spot, means we can't see what we can't see.

My daughter was quite surprised when this blind spot was pointed out to her. Fortunately, her husband, having set up a new office in their home during COVID, had become an invisible bystander to the conversations between his 2-year-old and wife. He was able to point this out because he had the opportunity to *slow down* and notice. This alone enabled them to help their son develop skills to deal with those negative feelings and for them to avoid pushing his buttons – unless, of course, it's really, really funny.

Another common blind spot, one I see a lot, is parents' propensity to find excuses when their children behave badly. Maybe their child is teething, maybe they're bored or maybe they're tired. Making excuses inevitably backfires because most of the time the children are actually trying really hard to get through to their parents about something that doesn't feel good for them. It's not ideal when a child can only communicate their discontent by playing up. If they can't get through to us calmly, then they will try other ways to get our attention. Excusing poor behaviour and not being aware of what they are actually trying to tell us are the main problems here, not the child's behaviour.

It's imperative to spend undivided time with your child getting to really know them and understand their cues. The child who bites and hits isn't a bad kid. They are trying to tell us something. So if you have a child who is playing up, it's time to ask yourself WHAT are they feeling? WHY do they feel that way? HOW can we make them understand they are still valued and important even though they just got reprimanded? And how can we show them a better way to get what they want WHEN they feel that way again.

You can do this with a child of any age who is acting out of character. It's just about being there for them, understanding and hearing them and not ignoring them when they behave badly.

You might not always get it right. But you can't keep excusing your child. For example, if they are biting and hitting others you will have to find out how to get through to them in a way that makes them stop. Stopping now, and not after ten more attempts at hurting others, is the best way as far as I can tell. Some kids just need a conversation, others might need more. When you know your child's nature you will know what to do.

Whichever training method you need to use to stop allowing your child to hurt others begins with gaining their undivided attention. Next, try to find out what just happened. This goes a long way for them to feel understood and valued. They may have been hurt first – find out. If you get this right, they will see it's their behaviour you have a problem with, not them. And they'll realise you still love them and want to help them work things out. Soon, they realise there is no need for acting out once they learn how to deal better with expressing their feelings.

Kind and nice are great things to learn

We all want amazing children as well as clever and happy ones but we shouldn't forget the lifelong benefits of bringing up children who are nice and kind as well. Guiding and teaching your children to be well-grounded, considerate people is great parenting. Teaching your child how to behave nicely is actually the kindest and most loving thing you can do for them. As you can see, achieving this comes down to observing and leading your child in the right direction so that having concern for you and others soon becomes second nature to them.

Change thinking

Are you aware of what motivates you to do one thing rather than another? For example, do you automatically accept the cards you're dealt in life, sometimes just coping and possibly feeling a bit sorry for yourself? Many people become resigned to just 'not being happy' with their life. That is sad because life is actually short and you will feel as though you missed a lot of opportunities to be happy later down the track if you don't, or feel you can't, do anything about that.

Once you see the value in doing whatever it takes to have a full and rewarding life, you can then focus on making the best possible decisions about which cards you play. If this question raises your awareness about how you may be limiting yourself, then I'm glad I asked it.

I'm grateful for the difference this kind of awareness has made in my life and I know it is available to everyone. Your life does not ever have to be at the mercy of others. Even having children to care for does not mean you have no other option but to be doing whatever it is that stops you feeling empowered. The quality of life for you and your children depends on the level of your happiness. The thing is that it's up to us to choose better options if our life is not on the path we want.

Our attitude has a lot to do with our happiness level and must not be overlooked or considered unimportant. Choosing positivity over merely coping can magically turn a situation from problematic to interesting. You can decide to be curious or lighthearted or fun.

It all comes down to our ability to change our thoughts. I was a late learner and it was an Anthony Robbins' 'Date with Destiny' that opened my mind and allowed me to make the choices I needed to be a happy parent for my children.

Having this awareness changed my life and motivated me to become a coach. I wanted every other person I met to have the confidence to create a great life for themselves. I especially wanted single mums to realise that being a 'single mum' can be a liberating experience and a lot of fun. I used to take overseas Homestay students to help with paying bills and eventually turned that into a business as well. Happy Homestay gave me an opportunity to be home with my children after school and visit other families during the day. Look hard enough and you'll always find a way to get through things as I did.

Trust me, you do not have to feel stuck. You can have an amazing life as long as you don't ever give up or put up with disrespect from anybody, especially people you love – and that includes your children. You can teach your children to enjoy life and be happy and well in the knowledge the world is an amazing place, full of love and kindness – and that this love and kindness begins at home.

Changing our thoughts can be a bit challenging at first but with practice it will soon become a new habit that empowers you to make better decisions because you have taken the time to think things through. Looking at problems as opportunities and seeing things from a possibility's perspective is transformational.

To change the way we think, and therefore the result we get, we need to 'reprogram' our minds, basically forming new neural pathways. We do this by both thinking and acting differently. The beauty of being human is that after a few conscious attempts to change, new pathways can soon form and, in no time at all, our new behaviour becomes a new and better habit.

Why not pause for a moment and think about your self-talk? This is important because the things we say to ourselves affects our mood and how we feel about ourselves at least as much as, if not more than, the things other people say to us. Being aware of where we've become stuck in old ways of thinking can be life-changing. It helps us to see whether or not we are creating our own problems most of the time.

Remember, we don't stop learning when we leave school or college. Everyday life delivers lessons. We are always learning about life and hopefully about how to be the best we can be. This all helps us become more conscious and even better parents. It's important we believe in ourselves. This can be a little difficult to pull off if we're not also consciously trying to grow and evolve. Always trying to be our best as an evolved human makes achieving our goals so much easier than if we have a negative mindset where we're always unconsciously sabotaging ourselves or beating ourselves up.

A great exercise to raise your awareness and become more conscious of the qualities that matter to you and your family is to sit down with your kids and write a list. What would your list of essentials look like?

Here's what we came up with when I did this important exercise with my family:

- Kindness towards family, friends and others
- Appreciation for what others do for us
- Gratitude for things we are given
- Courage and strength to push through life's challenges
- Compassion for ourselves and others
- Good manners – always
- Respect for others and especially the people you love
- Consideration and helpfulness
- Qualities of a good friend
- Respect for our home and personal space
- Defend ourselves, the ones we love and strangers if required
- Celebration of the wins of others – with no jealousy
- Appreciation of nature
- Understanding our part in the bigger picture
- Always being there for family

Family meetings are a great way to begin your list. Like me, I know you will be astounded when you hear what matters to your children and what they come up with. It's then that you realise how 'in tune' with animals and nature your children really are. All it takes is for you to make the time and opportunity for all this to be revealed.

CHAPTER 11: LEARNING

We have precious wealth from our ancient times.
— Tu Youyou

It almost goes without saying that the times we live in are marked by a proliferation of screen-based technology. I'm starting with this statement because it's extremely important and beneficial for all of us to find ways to balance screen time with the other ways children can learn about the world and their place in it. Among other things, this entails not caving into pressure or allowing your kids to disappear off into cyberspace when they could be hanging out with you, bonding and having fun.

When families limit their children's time on social media and video games and push them a little by encouraging them to help in the home and take an interest in the real world, they will be happier, more capable and engaging. Numerous studies back this up. Whether it's walking the dog, reading a book or cooking and preparing meals with the family, these are all nice nurturing things to do and everyone benefits. Just as we looked at your potential personal blockages, it's now time to see where your children may be holding themselves back from enjoying the family and life in general.

It may sound crazy but I want you to think about restricting screen time to less than 2 hours a day. I recommend this because the stats are out and any more than 3 hours a day is a recipe for disaster in many areas of our lives, not in the least our mental health.

If you don't recognise the importance of this, then I don't think you are seeing things clearly. My children watched television, much to the dismay of the school they attended, but they jumped up for the adventure at any suggestion of: Hey, let's ... Remember one thing – it's all in the sales job. Make washing the dog, weeding the garden or heading out the shops for milk sound fun. Make it fun. Empty promises won't work for long.

As you know, social media, PlayStation games and YouTube in particular, are addictive for our children. Need I say more? Your child may rebel at first but not taking charge of this is too important to ignore. You are likely to wind up with a moody child who has little or no life skills, and no interest in the real world. And their self-esteem will definitely take a knock as a result of constantly comparing themselves, often unfavourably, with all of the fake images and 'perfect' lives that people, young women in particular, seem addicted to posting on social media that are just not real.

What's more, not being able to put a phone down has become an addiction for many parents, and anyone else who owns a phone for that matter. I want you to pause for a moment and consider what addictive behaviours your child is likely to adopt because they notice you constantly with a phone in your hand or on a laptop for entertainment when you could be having fun together with your kids.

There are so many fresh ideas that are actually old ideas that have worked for parents in Australia for many generations – long before Google was created to help us.

Don't get me wrong, I love technology. It allowed me to see my grandson take his first steps even though he was doing that in the UK and I get to blow him kisses goodnight and sing him lullabies to get him to sleep.

Let's give credit where its due but I just hate how technology is dividing up families who used to sit together watching *Home and Away* every night before bed and the Sunday night movies after a bath and a BBQ dinner.

These days though, Mum's on the iPad, Dad's on the iPhone, the kids are on the PlayStation or killing enemies on their iPad mini wrapped in the tough rubber purple cover.

Worse still, a mum used to look into her baby's eyes when breastfeeding but now she's 'Googling' to see if she's doing it right. Parents used to seek out advice from their parents and grandparents but now their advice has been superseded by the current parenting tips which include the latest research on brain development which changes constantly BTW.

I look around and with all this technology and advice, I do not see happy families who are benefiting from all this advancement. I see stress, anxiety, confusion and a lot of conflicting ideas, none of which anyone can stick to because there's a later version that's faster and has more 'likes' out soon.

Let me replace all that, let me be your modern day grandma who has been around long enough to see the changes that have occurred in families over the past three generations. I have integrated the best of the old and the new and I am proud to say that being Australian, loving equally our sense of fairness and our sense of humour, has made this journey a terrific ride and one I hope (if I have anything to do with it) will never be lost.

While I'm at it, living in Australia means you can be safe and free as long as you learn to take responsibility for yourself, understand what the boundaries are and develop self-control – and you can have a wonderful life full of sunshine and beaches, if that's what you want.

A change in technology behaviour is necessary for most of us and can be discussed in detail at the family meeting. You can begin by asking the children how many hours a day they'd like on screens if they were given all the freedom they want. They'd probably say 'all the time' – late at night, mornings, mealtimes and so on.

Make no mistake, too much screen time for you or your children, especially in each other's company, is giving children a taste for what addiction feels like. I often hear about parents who allow 4 to 6 hours of screen time a day, then complain their children are moody – or even worse – when they take the device away or ask them to turn it off. I do feel sorry for parents. It's deeply concerning to note what's happening under their very noses – and that they don't see it. It's the parents who must step up and help their children to stop the damaging consequences of this pattern.

On top of all this, you also need to think about the level of aggression portrayed as 'normal' on the internet – the pornography, the car wrecks and other horrendous, visually descriptive and horrifying scenes imprinting themselves on your child's mind. You can't unsee what you've seen. This can inhabit their dreams and cause them to be fearful of just being in the world.

The peace and quiet you get while your child is mesmerised by these distractions is not worth the long-term damage these habits cause in our kids. Setting precise boundaries around what your kids see, and strongly enforcing time limits on the amount of time they can access such situations, protects them and frees up their minds for a multitude of good possibilities.

The internet can be a great place for learning, but so too can hanging out with you, or a range of other options from family board games to walking in nature where there's a surprise around every corner.

Tell stories

So how can you be as much fun as a screen? I know this sounds like a very strange question but let's stretch our imaginations a bit here as there is a lot at stake. Not doing something about the amount of screen time our children have could create developmental, if not avoidable, mental health problems. Please don't let that happen to your children. Why wouldn't you step up if you can help avoid setting them up for a lifetime of misery? I know you love and adore your children, so take an active role in expressing your love by doing whatever it takes to protect them. You would never allow others to hurt them, so don't allow indifference to hurt them either.

To start getting everyone on board, tell your kids: We are opting for family connection and it's going to be a little tough at first – and then it will be a lifetime of enjoying people, instead of screens. After they finish complaining, say something like: You will thank me one day. It won't be easy at first as you're breaking a habit. You'll need to be creative and put your heart into it. But believe me, the alternative is not an option if you really do want a family who loves and cares for each other for a lifetime.

Sharing stories and challenges can be a great way to get the creative juices flowing and build up the part of the brain that could have become lazy from underuse. You can start, then someone else can finish. Have a time limit. It's also a great way to deepen connections within the family. You could try something simple like beginning a sentence with 'I bet you can't ...' and then challenge the children to finish it. If they don't jump in and respond, and let's be honest, they probably won't the first time you try it, you can finish the sentence in a funny way to get everyone laughing and 'losing themselves' to the fun of the moment. At the end of the day, even if they have forgotten, your children still adore you and want to be with you, especially when you are being the best version of you possible.

Learning to do the things you don't really want to do

I know we've covered this already, so I'll keep it short here. Learning definitely needs to include the importance of arming our children with the ability to do the things they don't particularly want to do. It's our job to guide them in a way that doesn't break their spirit, pointing them in the right direction towards vegetables rather than sweets and other options that are damaging in the long term, even though they seem like a good idea at the time.

With these little insights comes the need to learn self-control. Those kids who find it hard may see this as boring but, in fact, self-control is the gift you teach your children that enables them to enjoy life without getting lost in the harmful parts. Not many people are happy with an ordinary or boring life. A one-off treat on a rare occasion can break the boredom and make us feel a little spoilt.

Teaching our babies and children self-control

Teaching babies self-control can begin as early as 5 or 6 months of age. It's true – I have done this many times. Let's take a quick look at the myriad of situations where an infant is priming their brain to eventually be able to make wise decisions about doing things that are in their best interests.

- Staying still when their nappy is being changed
- Sleeping at the same time every day and going to bed at a reasonable hour
- Sitting still in their highchair to eat every time
- Eating greens and all the other veggies you serve
- Getting into the pram and staying in it
- Happily being held by others, not just Mum
- Giving up their dummy
- Listening to a story and sitting still
- Sitting still on your lap when you need them to
- Getting into the car seat and having a belt put on without complaining
- Putting on a bib and not taking it off
- Lying on their tummy for a period every day
- Wearing a jacket if told to – without complaint

These small moments in an infant's day can set off tears and a struggle (for both mum and bub) dozens of times a day. You should not have to put up with all that time-consuming nonsense because it's draining and stressful. It's important to help young children to understand that in life there are things we don't always want to do but that still have to be done.

The 'learning' that babies do around lying on their stomach, for example, goes way beyond the question of boosting their gross motor skills and building their muscles and balance so they will be able crawl. It goes right to the heart of self-control, as does learning they are okay when they let go of mum and go to others. As mums, we almost weaken our children because of our desire to feel loved and wanted. We can even shut out our husband's love to feel this wider love which doesn't help anyone – but that's another story. It's absolutely critical to our child's development that they learn to trust us and through their confidence in us to then be able to mix more happily with others as they grow up.

So, while the dot points you just read may have seemed somewhat inconsequential, together they begin the absolutely critical job of bringing up happy, well-adjusted children who then become a joy to be with – all the time.

I remember how upset I felt when Vanessa was tiny and fought against being strapped into the car seat as if her life depended on it – as it did. Of course, I always insisted but, believe it or not, I have worked with a mother who negotiated with her 2-year-old, settling for one strap around one arm. I have seen some crazy parenting but leaving a child so vulnerable in this situation was more than I could ignore. Still, that is how weakened parents can become if the children are ruling the roost and lack firm boundaries.

That child could be killed or scarred for life if there was a car accident, but the mother could only think about dealing with that moment at hand – and the next, and the next. This is no way to parent, in 'survival mode'. That is why it's vitally important to reduce as much unnecessary 'carry on' and challenging of your authority as humanly possible.

Stop parenting with fear and stress. You need to have outrageous trust in yourself if you are to get this right. I understand that everything may feel as though it's against you right now. It's harder being a parent these days. Most parents give in to their kids, especially in public, so it seems normal. There's also so much 'giving in' that is hard to understand, though I suspect it's something to do with all the fearful information around us.

Many parents are also convinced that their children are so fragile that they fear being told 'no' would damage their child's self-esteem. It doesn't make sense. It's not hearing 'no' that damages children in so many ways. The proof is all around us with the number of anxious, out-of-control kids, teens and even grown-up children constantly falling back on their parents for support.

How I parented my children, as a single mum, was exactly the way I am sharing with you now. Parenting like this works like magic. My children were very happy and adventurous kids as a result of this parenting, and are now among the top 1% of happy, kind, productive and loving adults on the planet. See, I do like statistics after all. What I'm sharing with you here works and it can restore your sanity. It rounds your children's lives and their future selves. More than this, their presence goes on to impact all the people those kids come in contact with and most importantly, it impacts your family life.

I have helped babies and children for close to forty years now and have been given more love and affection than any human could ever want. I put this down to the fact that children love to know what they need to do so they don't feel frustrated all the time. Honestly, you have to teach them every little thing, and yes, this process takes patience and can seem boring at times as you seek to put in place strong boundaries. But I promise, if you put in the time now, the rest of your time as a parent will be more joyous and fun than you could imagine – forever.

When your children respect you and feel your intense love and devotion, they really, really love hanging out with you. And what's even better is they have each other and a whole team of people who they can lean on and rely on for their whole lives too.

If you take control of your leadership abilities and don't cave in, don't accept whining and bullying, then you can parent without feeling overwhelmed and stressed a lot of the time. These factors alone make you a better parent. You and the way you think will be relaxed and not on edge or fearful.

At the end of the day, how happily any of us choose to do the things we don't really want to do determines the degree of happiness and success we are going to achieve through our lives. This is just as true for very little children learning about the world and their place in it, day by day, as it is for us adults.

So, don't for a moment think you're no good at being a mum because you can't get the baby into the car seat without tears. Perhaps if you spend some time prior to outings in the car, explaining you will be putting them in the car soon and there is no need to cry because then … get them excited about what happens at the other end.

Then say: Okay darling, promise Mummy, no tears today? When they smile, say: Yay, that's my little angel. Make sure you look proud and happy. When you take them in the car, talk them through what's going to happen. If they carry on, just say: Uh-uh, no, stop. Remember what you told Mummy? No tears today. You will be surprised what happens. You may have to do it a couple of times. Once again, the trick here is to be persistent and take the steps I just explained.

The effort you put in every single day as a mum or dad is simply teaching your child about how the world works. To get yourself conscious and attentive enough to do all this, remember these three sharp short tips:

- WAKE UP and open your eyes to see what's really happening.
- SLOW DOWN and arrange to stop arranging.
- TAKE CHARGE and have your children doing what you want, not the other way around.

Your children can do whatever they want when they are the leader of their family. It's your turn now. When your children are carrying on, or kicking and screaming, this is how you know what areas need your attention.

An infant can be encouraged with a little excitement, a happy song and a confident hand. At first, you may get more tears or louder complaints as you're helping them learn but in no time at all, they'll realise that's just the way it is and stop challenging you.

Finding courage to insist on the things your baby or child doesn't want to do won't make them love you any less. In fact, I've seen time and time again that the opposite is true. This is how we create good habits for life for our children. Parenthood is a long journey as we graduate from potty training to teaching them how to tie up their shoelaces to teaching the art of dealing with difficult conversations to suffering through boring classes without being disruptive and finally to putting themself forward for a promotion at work.

Learning how to do all of these things is important, and none more so than learning how to feel okay about doing things you would rather not do. If you're prepared to turn up and teach and guide your children through all of this, then you are giving them a real advantage in life. That's the gift of self-discipline we hopefully received from our parents and are now passing on to our children as we teach them as much as we can possibly impart. Qualities such as patience, the ability to handle disappointment and the joy of anticipation, along with other character-building traits, are how we arm our children to be able to cope in the real world.

Correcting bad behaviour nicely

The fact is that simple everyday acceptable behaviours are not automatically known by our kids. They need to learn them. It takes time, effort and patience to get them on board. Harder still when they're exposed to the bad behaviour displayed by other kids they're interacting with who haven't been taught how to behave properly.

So even when your kids complain about having to toe the line, which they will, you need to hold the line. When your child is doing something that needs urgent attention, like running across a busy street or hurting someone else, you need to really step up in the moment and immediately do whatever needs to be done. You may have to raise your voice as loud as possible or physically stop the offending behaviour because not doing that would likely end up with someone getting hurt.

In situations like these it is definitely not the time to explain what the child needs to do in your sweetest, most convincing voice and hoping not to offend them. However, when everything settles down, you should have an age-appropriate conversation with them about what they did wrong and what they should do next time instead. While the fact that their behaviour was unacceptable is not up for negotiation, you should still ask them what motivated them to behave as they did. Getting to the bottom of this and finding out what's driving the behaviour will enable you to empathise with them and encourage them to work towards a better outcome next time. Role-playing is also fun and can help in situations where words just don't suffice

It's all about teaching your children different and better ways to get their needs met. I appreciate you might still be learning how to handle things like this yourself – nobody warned us that being a parent meant being on such a steep learning curve – but because of this, I would like you to pause for a moment and think about the following questions.

- Do you look and act stressed all the time?
- Are you saying one thing and meaning another?
- Are you only half present when you are with your children?

Your answers to these questions matter, because your child may not know how to express themselves in words. If a child is acting up, you may find it's because they are begging for your attention. So, here is another one of those uncomfortable questions for you to consider:

> *Is your child getting 100% of your attention when you're angry with them, but having to share you with a text message or something on YouTube the rest of the time?*

Can you see how this pattern only reinforces wrong behaviour?

The bottom line is that children who are given positive attention and lots of one-on-one time with parents who help them understand what they need to do and how they need to do it, will have more confidence and be able to deal with challenges as they move through life. You will have helped them learn all this by your explanations and by modelling these behaviours yourself.

Teaching life skills

Using 'what if' statements to get the kids thinking is possible after the age of two. If you start speaking to your child with 'what if' statements, you will notice it helps them rely on you less, think for themselves a little more and start to understand there are things they do have choices about.

'What if' statements sound like this:

- What if I touched that hot iron? What would happen?
- What if I didn't take the rubbish out? What would happen?
- What if I wiggled and looked around while you were trying to tell me something? How would that make you feel?
- What if someone was being mean to you? What would you do?

You could also help by prompting them with possible solutions:

- What if you couldn't find your shoes in the hallway? Could you start remembering

where you were when you took them off and then go and get them?
- What if your sister wants something you have? Would it be possible to lend it to her if she asked you and promised to bring it back? Or could you tell her when you'll be finished with it and give it to her then?
- What if you don't like all your dinner? Could you try to eat at least some of everything because you know we made it for you and it's going to help your body grow?
- What if someone accused you of something you didn't do? What would you do? Would you cry? What would you say? Would you tell that person you didn't do it?

'What if' questions help your children stretch their brains and teach them how to communicate while learning to become thoughtful human beings and knowing how to think about possibilities. It's never too early to understand that your actions affect others, so learning how to be thoughtful about them is necessary and helps your children grow into considerate adults.

Teaching life skills is far more important than teaching anything else. The world is a complex place, as are the people in it. How we negotiate our way through all the challenges we face on a daily basis is easier and more enjoyable if we can learn as much as possible about how everything works when we're young. It all begins with teaching our children some basic skills, such as self-awareness, dealing with disappointment, forgiveness, flexibility, courage, strength, resilience, patience and, not least of all, the joy of anticipation.

More often than not, children have limited time with their parents. Busy and stressed parents find it quicker and easier to do things for their children rather than taking the time to teach them how to do things themselves. It's easy to get into this habit. The problem with this approach is that if we continue to do things for our children that they are capable of doing themselves, we create lazy, unmotivated kids which ultimately makes their lives and our ours more difficult than necessary.

It's time to get organised and set some priorities. Not only will this help on a logistical level but it will also teach your children how to get organised themselves. For a household to work effectively, when children come home from school, they need to settle down and do all the things that must be done, such as homework, hair washing, cooking, eating, washing up after dinner and preparing for the following day. Doing this in an organised way will relieve morning stresses.

It's a great idea to give your children checklists to tick off each night before they have access to all the things they want to do just for fun. Learning how to be organised may be more challenging than you think. However, even if it takes up the whole evening in the beginning, it will soon make things a lot easier.

Getting organised works best if you make lists to cover every fine detail, right down to where headbands need to be put so they're easy to find in the morning. Being able to predict how the day will begin without calamity will take a whole lot of pressure off an otherwise stressful part of daily life. What's more, having time to get lunchboxes into bags, put pyjamas away, make beds and so on helps children feel more capable and responsible as well as less argumentative when you ask them to do something.

As I mentioned earlier, doing things for children they can do for themselves doesn't serve anyone. Better parenting involves teaching children how to do these tasks for themselves with a great attitude. There's a definite benefit for children who are capable, and spoiled kids whose parents are essentially their slaves miss out on this. The benefit is the confidence that comes with being capable of getting life's tasks, however menial, done well. Kids who are never actually taught how to do these kinds of things are more likely to unconsciously re-enact that story of 'dependence' in other areas of their life. These 'un/lucky' children, whose parents are more like servants, miss out on feeling calm and competent. This is a wonderful gift we give to our children when we teach them how to do the mundane things in life.

As children are incapable of seeing the big picture, what they don't know is that if you continue to do everything for them, they won't ever feel competent or have true self-worth. The beauty of raising little humans is that when they learn something new they get a sense of accomplishment. Feeling capable drives kids to want to learn more. The habits we help our children learn early on may turn them into some of the happiest adults around. For the record, the happiest adults I know identify themselves as lifelong learners.

It makes me sad to think that the joy of learning is a really underestimated and not seen as an opportunity to feel good about ourselves. Here's a list of basic things I believe are important for your children to know.

- When you knock something off a chair or table, please pick it up and put it back.
- If you accidentally bump into or hurt another person, always say sorry and let them know you didn't mean to do it.
- When a person says hello or smiles at you, it's nice to say hello back, look them in the eye and smile to let them know you appreciate they are being nice to you.

- When you're with your parents and one of their friends or relatives want to speak to you, don't run away. Listen to them and respond nicely.
- If someone is walking towards you and wants to walk past you, move aside a little to let them pass.
- When you're eating a meal at the table, don't wiggle and jiggle around, keep your feet off the table and keep your food on the plate that is given to you.
- If you drop something, pick it up.
- When you take a toy out of your toy box, put it back when you finish playing with it.
- When you play with other children, don't snatch toys off them.
- Don't let other children snatch toys off you.
- If someone is being mean to you, ask them to stop. If they don't, tell your adult.
- If you feel unhappy because you thought of something that made you sad, you can talk to your adult about it. Or you can take three big breaths or try to cheer up with a little song, by reading a book or by doing some star jumps to take your mind off it.
- Try to think about other people as well as yourself.
- Don't hurt people or animals.
- Show a dog the back of your hand before you try to pat it.
- When you do something you didn't mean to do, or even if you did it on purpose and are

feeling sorry now, let the person know you are sorry as you are looking them in the eye.
- If you need Mummy or Daddy to do something for you, don't yell from another room. Come and ask politely. If they are busy, wait. Be patient.
- Don't give up easily. When things are tricky, say to yourself: I can do this.
- If someone is bullying you, find your loud voice, look into their eyes and say: Don't say/do that.
- Help your family unpack groceries.
- Hang up your wet towel instead of leaving it on the floor.
- Take your lunch box and anything wet out of your school bag when you get home.
- If you don't agree with somebody, don't be rude. Always speak nicely.
- If your parents say stop – stop immediately.
- Never be mean to your siblings.

There are myriad ways children can unconsciously be doing the wrong thing and it is important to teach them these so you don't need to yell when they get it wrong. If you do not teach your kids how to do things properly, then who will?

CHAPTER 12: LOVE

> *... we are all inextricably connected to each
> other by a power greater than all of us ...
> our connection to the power and to one another
> is grounded in love and compassion.*
> — Brené Brown

Love is the most important thing

Love is the most important thing but it is not everything. Don't we just love our children to bits? How do we show this? And how do we teach our children to show love?

All parents start out with the best intentions, doing everything they can for their children and hoping they'll feel loved. This is where the problems start. Giving a child everything they want and doing everything for them is not what parenting love is all about. Parenting this way is actually a little lazy and can often be driven by weakness, guilt or even fear. Children need your time and attention to feel loved. No matter how many bright shiny things you give them, or how much you do for them, what they really want and need more than anything is you. I know it's not easy with all the demands that you're dealing with on a daily basis.

Reorganising your time may be necessary, though, so you can carve out time to 'just be' with your kids. A simple smile, a pat on the back, a wink or quick hug will do wonders to brighten everyone's day. I find many parents do this quite naturally. Some, however, only do this for the first 18 months or so. Interestingly, this is when things seem to go off the rails as the challenging behaviours of this tricky age begin to take over. As exhaustion and frustration follows, many find it hard to enjoy this stage of their child's development.

I remember the first time Vanessa stood her ground at this age and refused to do what I asked. I actually had no idea what to do. I was shocked. All of a sudden, my little angel was getting a mind of her own.

However, the strong bond and 'do whatever it takes' love your child gets from you is the most important thing you bring to your relationship with them. It's the strength of your commitment to that love that smooths over the rough bits and helps your child bounce back quickly. Despite any disagreements they may have had with you, your child feels unconditionally loved by the most important person in their life.

Now is the perfect time to start teaching your children how to behave nicely.

When Vanessa was born, the midwife told me that cuddles mean more than anything else. Hearing that was really helpful. The truth of it is we all need cuddles through our lives and I encourage you to give them freely, even if there appears to be no particular reason to do so. If your child tries to break free or push you away, don't let them. Even if your child doesn't realise it at the moment, we all need to be hugged.

If you let your child break away, they miss out on your affection and start to believe they can make decisions about what they can do, knowing you want them to do something else. When this happens, children think they can make other decisions about what they can do, even if it's against your wishes. Children need to feel your love and your strength as often as possible.

Your child loves you more than anything and although they don't always show it they want to be reassured that whatever they may do to upset you, you are still going to love them. Children are very tactile. They want to be hugged, kissed, ruffled up and physically shown how much you love them every day. This is an incredibly important aspect of your relationship with them. No matter what age they are, they never grow out of being your child.

CHAPTER 12: LOVE

When your child is angry and shouts that they hate you, all you need to do is calmly say: But I love you. Then you can pretend to growl or pull a face that says: I love you, even though you're being a bit unreasonable right now. Even if you have a teenager who keeps pushing you away, you need to find the courage to grab them and hold them close because they need hugs and cuddles from you now more than ever. Tell them: I know you hate it but I need a cuddle, NOW. In a playful sort of way, show them you're the boss by challenging them to an arm wrestle or tell them you're going to hold them down in a boisterous game. Before you know it, you'll all be rolling around and having fun.

I had my son convinced that I could beat him in an arm wrestle until he was almost fifteen but it took a lot of mind games and determination on my part. By the time he was seventeen, he realised that he could start playfully challenging me as well.

Basically do whatever works to get them to give in, laughing. They may say you're mad, crazy or not cool but when they look back on this in years to come, they'll smile and remember how much love you had in your heart for them. And they'll recognise that the years haven't diminished this love one little bit.

Words are important, but sometimes they are not enough. Physical contact and a loving look release happy hormones and healing chemicals into our bodies and are the best ways to develop a lifelong loving relationship. My advice is to never stop hugging your beautiful children and never stop congratulating yourself for setting up something as wonderful as the relationship you have with your children.

Showing your children how to feel loved gives them a huge advantage in life. Some adults, we know, have been so distanced from that feeling that they can find it hard to show their kids how much they care. Don't let that be you. You can break that family cycle and reach out for help if you need it.

More than anything else, our kids need to feel our love so they are able to create relationships with others. Most children find it quite easy to make friends but some children find it difficult. Either way, children usually need some tips, either explicit instructions, or good modelling.

Try these steps with your child.

1. Go up to some friendly looking kids in a group.
2. Hang around for a while, watching them. Make sure you smile.
3. If someone looks at you, say: Hello.
4. Ask if you can join in.
5. Speak to the kids who look at you and ask them how to play.

6. If the kids get up and run around, run with them
7. Sit next to any child who is alone at lunchtime.

The etiquette for friendships is the same for kids as it is for adults:

- Be friendly
- Don't be bossy
- Don't push in
- Respond when someone talks to you
- Listen to others
- Share and be nice
- Laugh with others

These simple details, and whatever else you can think of, help your child make friends and is also what great parenting is about.

One more thing about love – are you showing your children what a loving relationship looks like? Are you and your partner spending time together without the children and taking time to really enjoy each other's company? So often, I see mums and dads raising children together and being completely disconnected. One day your children will leave home but the relationship you have with your partner is meant to be for the rest of your life.

I see many mums making all the decisions to do with the children with little or no regard for the father's opinion. Most fathers are as capable as the mother – fathers are just winging it too. It's vitally important you get on the same page when it comes to parenting. The last thing you need when raising your children is a disengaged father. Like you, your partner needs to be considered – just as much, if not more, than the children are. Both of you need to feel respected and loved if your family is to thrive. Lots of partners feel as if their mutual love and affection died when the children came along.

Sometimes you may need to talk about how you communicate with each other so you don't get tangled up in misunderstandings. When mum and dad are not on the same parenting page, everyone suffers. Children feel safe when they can see their parents loving and happy together.

CONCLUSION

I'm proud of you. You've made it this far. [Thunderous clapping] Now you have fifty per cent of the solution. It's possible, on some level, you already knew most of what I've written here. There isn't anything all that tricky or complicated about bringing up conscious kids. All you really need to do is look after yourself, manage your kids, continue loving them to bits and be open to change when necessary.

Being tolerant is a virtue but not if it goes too far and turns into resentment. With discernment, you will know how to respond to every situation and see reality rather than denial.

Remember this: your life is being kidnapped if you settle for 'putting up with'. You deserve a great life. If you decide to focus on family, health, fun times, cooperation and feelings of inclusiveness, then that's a great way to live. As we know, none of this happens by accident. It's only when you find the courage to do whatever it takes to be the parent every member of the family respects and adores. When everyone, including each adult, understands what they need to do, and feels acknowledged, supported and appreciated, that's when you have a life worth living.

I'm confident that when you connect with your family with something as simple as weekly family meetings, everyone will bond, communicate and contribute without anyone feeling the need to buck the system any longer.

Always remember that life is one big opportunity to learn and grow. It's never going to be perfect but with these new skills in place you could get close. I know your children and your relationship will blossom when all the stress and anxiety are replaced with lighthearted connection.

The strategies I've shared work wonders for all parents who are willing to remember to *wake up, slow down* and *take charge*. Your parenting will be exciting and enjoyable because now you know what it takes to make that happen.

Life within a family does not have to be serious all the time. It does, however, need to be predictable so we are not putting out fires all day. Having humour and good-hearted firmness helps you enjoy teaching your children what is expected of them and allows them to respond to you nicely. Playing with our children's imagination and having fun while being together means kids will be less inclined to allow themselves to become out of control when things aren't going their way. Once they know how, you'll find your children 'want to be good'.

It's your choice whether you perk up and choose the better experience or stay stuck in a rut that you probably never saw coming. Resentment spoils everything. I see so many kids, and their parents, carrying resentment. When I sit down with them and question what it's all about, it often boils down to something quite insignificant that happened last year or something even further back that's not even relevant anymore.

That's how sticky a negative state like resentment can be. We have to stop sticking to automatic behaviours. We need to speak to our family members openly and with respect. We have to face our fears and be courageous. We all have our own unique nature but we can learn to connect in ways that talk to our children's nature while still respecting our own.

In closing, here's a reminder of the twenty things you can do today to create a happy family:

1. Be the parent you want your children to be when they have children.

2. Teach morals and virtues at every opportunity.
3. Play games together. If you let the children win, make sure they know you let them.
4. Never let your child speak rudely to you or be disrespectful in any way – ever.
5. Nip all unacceptable behaviour in the bud as soon as it begins.
6. Talk to your children before birth and from day one about how much you love them.
7. Make sure your child knows you are their leader and you know what you are doing.
8. Be a firm, calm, strong, loving leader who doesn't take crap from kids or anyone else.
9. Laugh every day – a lot. Be funny, make up stories and songs about the kids.
10. Don't make work more important than family.
11. Keep housework to a minimum; teach kids to pick up after themselves.
12. Try your best to be lighthearted and see the humour in life's trials.
13. Before you overreact, remember little people are watching and learning from you.
14. Give children age-appropriate freedom to make their own mistakes.
15. Plan fun things to do together but don't over-plan their lives.
16. Kids need downtime to relax and just hang out. So do you.

17. Stop all annoying behaviours before they become a habit.
18. Observe when your child is unusually quiet or sad – get to the bottom of it.
19. Invite friends over to your house and let the kids play and cook and enjoy their home.
20. Make a daily habit of being grateful that you have each other.

I wish you all the very best in being that parent your children want AND need you to be.

I invite you to join me at www.sharoncullington.com to get up-to-date information and support while you're on this wonderful journey of being a parent.

*When a flower doesn't bloom,
you fix the environment in which it grows,
not the flower.*
— Alexander Den Heijer

www.ingramcontent.com/pod-product-compliance
Lightning Source LLC
Chambersburg PA
CBHW071956290426
44109CB00018B/2044